Every person, every Christian, is to some degree a product of his environment. Byron Yawn's concern is that Christians have been unwittingly and unduly influenced by the values and ideals of suburbia. Powerful gospel-centered Christianity has been replaced by impotent gospel-free suburbianity. Byron writes not as a sociologist but as a pastor, calling Christians to be shaped far more by the timeless Word of God and far less by the changing preferences of the suburbs. May every Christian heed this call!

Tim Challies
Christian blogger, pastor, and author

Suburbianity is one of the most refreshing and disturbing books I have read in quite a while. Refreshing because my friend Byron Yawn has managed to make the gospel even more attractive and alluring to me. Disturbing because he makes such a strong case for all the ways we tend to miss and "dis" the gospel by settling for much of what is accepted as conservative, Bible-believing Christianity. Byron doesn't write as a cynic, but as a man who longs to see his own heart, his congregation, and our culture come more fully alive to the grace and truth of the real gospel. This is a book for believers and non-believers alike because everybody needs the gospel Byron highlights.

Scotty Smith
Pastor, Christ Community Church
author of *Everyday Prayers* and *Restoring Broken Things*

Suburbianity is about the life-giving recovery of the most important reality in the world—the glorious gospel of the Lord Jesus Christ. Found herein is delightful refreshment to the weary soul bombarded by tireless pop-evangelical trendiness. Pastor Byron Yawn delivers a welcome mix of pointed sobriety, self-criticizing humility, and yes, even some gut-busting humor. I hope *Suburbianity* will produce a multitude of wonderfully dissatisfied Christians who will insist that pastors unashamedly and explicitly preach Christ rather than moralism masquerading as the eternal gospel. Everyone should read this profoundly Christian book. For the glory of Christ in the churches!

Patrick Abendroth
Pastor, Omaha Bible Church

D0110454

This is not a how-to or 12-step self-help book. Nor is it a book of character sketches from which to draw and apply life lessons in morality and ethics. If you have ever tried to bootstrap yourself into favor with God, read *Suburbianity*, and you'll approach Scripture differently. Instead of seeing the Bible as a series of stories, you'll discover the one story of Christ's finished work of redemption. And it will transform you.

Perry Stahlman
Chairman of the elders, Community Bible Church

*suburbianity

Byron Forrest Yawn

HARVEST HOUSE PUBLISHERS
EUGENE, OREGON

All Scripture quotations are taken from the New American Standard Bible®, © 1960, 1962, 1963, 1968, 1971, 1972, 1973, 1975, 1977, 1995 by The Lockman Foundation. Used by permission. (www .Lockman.org)

Cover by Dugan Design Group, Bloomington, Minnesota

Cover illustration © Pavlo Lutsan/Fotolia

SUBURBIANITY

Copyright © 2013 by Byron Forrest Yawn
Published by Harvest House Publishers
Eugene, Oregon 97402
www.harvesthousepublishers.com

Library of Congress Cataloging-in-Publication Data
Yawn, Byron Forrest.
Suburbianity / Byron Forrest Yawn.
     p. cm.
ISBN 978-0-7369-5041-1 (pbk.)
ISBN 978-0-7369-5042-8 (eBook)
1. Christian life—United States. 2. Suburbanites—United States—Religious life. I. Title.
BV4501.3.Y39 2013
248.409173'3—dc23
                                                                2012026969

All rights reserved. No part of this publication may be reproduced, stored in a retrieval system, or transmitted in any form or by any means—electronic, mechanical, digital, photocopy, recording, or any other—except for brief quotations in printed reviews, without the prior permission of the publisher.

Printed in the United States of America

13 14 15 16 17 18 19 20 21 / LB-JH / 10 9 8 7 6 5 4 3 2 1

To Jackie Stanford
A man without whom I would not be the man I am today
Thank you for showing me true friendship
Thank you for incessantly pushing all those you love
to the gospel of grace
Thank you for the innumerable phone calls on Sunday afternoon

*But I do not consider my life of any account as dear
to myself, in order that I may finish my course and
the ministry which I received from the Lord Jesus, to
testify solemnly of the gospel of the grace of God.*
ACTS 20:24

Within the American suburbs, countless unsuspecting and well-intended Christians miss Jesus on a weekly basis, if not daily. We read books, hear sermons, participate in Bible studies, and attend conferences that never get around to the particulars of who Jesus is and why He did what He did. We mention Him in passing but fail to fall at His feet. We merely assume everyone knows the realities that distinguish Him from every other human who ever walked the earth and that make Him so much more than merely an example to follow. This means the majority of what we think is Christian is not. Without the crucified Savior, it is not Christianity. The gospel is a mere ticker running harmlessly beneath our Christian life. We assume it's there and press on. We completely misunderstand the Christian life in the process of attempting to live it. The gospel *is* the Christian life. It is what allows us to live it.

Contents

Introduction

I am a product of the American suburbs. Imperceptibly and relentlessly, this ever-expanding ring of American progress lying between the urban center and rural boundaries of our metro areas has shaped all of my existence. What I see and know of life is almost exclusively defined by the values that arise from this corridor of American life. Happiness, success, contentment, marriage, family, money, and career have all been defined by the suburbs. My perception of reality is primarily suburban.

Generally, I've been raised to assume that the best life a person can know is measured by the square footage of a home that's near the best conveniences and products America has to offer. It is, after all, the American dream. To strive for anything less than this is aimless (or nearly tragic.) Life is about being successful and settling down into suburban bliss. It's what we do. In the strangest twist of American ideals, we strive throughout life to carve out a brief moment at the end to finally live. It's a maddening circle of life.

Many Americans flee to the suburbs to escape severe urban contexts or stark rural ones. The suburbs are geographic and psychological buffer zones that offer safety from such things as violent crime and boredom. We have evaded urban influences that so easily jade the human psyche and threaten our preferred way of life. We drive in to work and out to live. The suburbs are safe.

Recently, more than one contentious Christian observer has noted the serious error in our logic. The suburbs are not safe at all. They are actually dangerous. We assumed that compared to the city, the suburbs are compatible with Christian ideals and less damaging to the human soul. We were wrong. In many real ways, the suburbs are far more hazardous than cities with higher crime rates. The suburbs are treacherous. Especially for Christians. The suburbs are possibly the hardest places on earth for the gospel to take hold. The true gospel, that is.

There is much about who I am as an American that is opposed to who I am as a Christian. Regardless of what I have believed, the best of American ideals are not fundamentally Christian. In many instances they are diametrically opposed to the essence of Christianity. You cannot blend the two and retain Christianity. You cannot confuse them and remain faithful. They are not the same.

I've come to realize over many years as a pastor in the suburbs that American ideals and Jesus's teachings are locked in a constant battle for my devotion. Our hearts suffer the invariable upheaval of unrelenting coups. My Christian faith is forever being overthrown by my adoration of the American dream. I battle to pry the American part of me off of the Christian part of me. The suburbs wreak havoc on the Christian faith. They affect every essential aspect of Christianity, including how I understand the gospel, read my Bible, and view the church.

The American Dream Is Not the Issue

I want to make it clear from the beginning that I do not think America or its ideals are the problem with American Christians. Whether I live in the city or the suburbs is irrelevant in the greater scope of the gospel. The gospel transcends both. Besides, Christianity does not remove individuals from their particular contexts. Rather, it redeems people in those contexts and redeploys them as missionaries. From here the citizens-turned-missionaries are able to navigate the cultural nuances and speak truth into the contexts in which they live. This is not a rant against organized religion or American capitalism.

The American dream has proved a legitimate pursuit for innumerable hardworking American Christians. I do not begrudge them.

They are not wrong in their pursuit of happiness. Many have been able to maintain a sincerity of faith while flying American flags on their porches. Nothing is inherently wrong with being wealthy or successful. Wealth and success do present challenges to a life of faith, but to assume that rejecting capitalism will remedy the problems in America is superficial at best. I'm not the least bit ashamed that I personally benefit from the many blessings this country provides. (I'm not giving up my iPhone.)

Rather, the problem with being Christians in America is that we tend to confuse one for the other. When we cannot differentiate between that which is of Christ and that which is of Uncle Sam, we have no way of knowing which we are worshipping.

I expect that most suburban Christians are like me, struggling to tell the difference between what is generally American and what is actually Christian. Or what is vaguely spiritual and what is actually biblical. Or what is merely moral and what is specifically godly. This confusion is a central concern in this book. Making sense of it all is not as easy as you think. Consider the following statements.

> The Bible is not a spiritual handbook.
> Morality is not a Christian worldview.
> Family values are not synonymous with Christianity.
> Christianity is spiritual, but spirituality is not necessarily Christian.
> Humanitarianism is not the chief aim of the church.
> Christianity is not about being happy but does result in joy.
> You cannot find God's will for your life (in the popular sense) in the Bible.
> Being a Christian is not about being a good person.
> You will not have your best life in this existence.
> God may not want you to be rich. He may want you to be poor.
> Wealth is not a sign of God's favor.

The church does not grow as a result of strategic planning.

Most contemporary Christian music isn't.

Many Christian books aren't.

You don't need Jesus to be happy.

Struggling with sin is a normal part of the Christian life.

Moral or affluent people need the gospel just as much as immoral or poor people.

America has never been a Christian nation.

The rich young ruler would not have been saved if he had sold everything.

Suffering is a normal part of life and not something to be escaped.

Preaching from the Bible doesn't ensure faithfulness to the Bible's message.

Austere living is not a sign of spiritual devotion.

The gospel is not about escaping hell or getting to heaven.

Culturally relevant messages are often disconnected from the actual point of the Bible.

God did not save you because you have intrinsic value.

Preaching about a need for biblical preaching is not biblical preaching.

There is no essential difference between local and world missions.

Vegetables can't sing.

You are not a better person for having become a Christian.

You should not pattern your life after Joseph, David, Daniel, or any other biblical character.

Jabez only wanted some land.

Church is not where you go to escape the influence of the world.

God does not love you more if you read your Bible and pray.

Sinners (even the worst you can imagine) are not your
enemies.

Church attendance is not a sign of faithfulness to Christ.

A Christian president will not save our country or the world.

"Having devotions" is not an indicator of spiritual discipline.

A moral majority threatens the heart of Christianity.

The best thing you can do for morally upright people is
assume they are lost.

Finding your purpose in life is not the most important
thing you can do.

Placing your faith in your parents' religion is damning.

Schooling choices are not signs of spirituality or good
parenting.

Freedom of religion may not be good for Christianity.

"Christian movies" has become a punch line.

Atheists can be good people too.

The gospel and Christ are left out of many church services.

Principles for living taken from the Bible are often distortions of the Bible.

Legislating morality is not helpful.

Knowing the gospel is not evidence of believing it.

No one has been a Christian his entire life.

Abortion is not what's wrong with America.

Jesus would be confused in many of our church services.

Christ is hard to find in most Christian bookstores.

Second Chronicles 7:14 has nothing to do with America.

Being angry at sinners for being sinners is not a sufficient
evangelism strategy.

I realize several items on this list appear sacrilegious to many conservative Americans and many suburban Christians. The impulse to debate them or question my orthodoxy for formulating such a list is to be expected. (Just so you know, I am not politically, socially, or religiously liberal or progressive. I am a poster child for conservative evangelicalism.)

As others have said, fish have no idea what water is unless they have been on a dock, in a boat, or washed up on a shore. Once you're forced out of your element, you realize what you've been swimming in. The gospel grabs suburbanites and drops them on the dock of objective truth. Then it tosses them back in the water. Through it they come to realize what they've been swimming in. This list can also have that kind of effect.

Obviously, my statements challenge closely held and passionately defended values of innumerable suburban Americans. Many of the items I included are essential to polite society. But they become problematic when they are mistaken as Christian. Truth be told, they are not. They are simply American.

The point of the list is obvious. Distinguishing between moral conservatism and biblical Christianity is nearly impossible for many who claim the name of Christ. As counterintuitive as my restatements may seem to many Christians, they are biblically accurate. That is, they can be defended from the Bible and are relatively easy to prove as true. You only need to open your Bible and start reading. I'll expand on a few of them in order to prove my point.

The Bible is not a spiritual handbook. The Bible is not a loosely connected set of stories and principles that serve as the primary resource for spiritually minded people. Obviously, the Bible is a spiritual book and powerfully facilitates change, but it is not the guide for Christian spiritualists. You should not be turning to your Bible merely for a spiritual boost at the beginning of your day. To approach it primarily as a spiritual-life handbook is to nearly miss its point altogether. As Jesus explained to His followers, the Bible is the account of Him.

The Bible is primarily the record and explanation of God's promise, fulfilled in Christ.

> Beginning with Moses and with all the prophets, He explained to them the things concerning Himself in all the Scriptures (Luke 24:27).

Morality is not a Christian worldview. Innumerable religions and secular worldviews promote and establish morality in their followers. Morality is not an exclusively Christian viewpoint. Christianity may lead to morality, but it does not begin with it. According to Jesus, morality as a goal of religion is as damning as immorality. Jesus came confronting the blinding effects of moralism on his culture, not encouraging them. To confuse morality with Christianity ultimately distorts Christianity.

> Beware of practicing your righteousness before men to be noticed by them; otherwise you have no reward with your Father who is in heaven (Matthew 6:1).

Family values are not synonymous with Christianity. Christianity certainly promotes the institution of the family, but a commitment to the defense and establishment of family values indicates nothing about one's position in Christ. Christians are not the only ones who value family. Furthermore, Jesus made clear that a devotion to family and devotion to Him can be at odds.

> If anyone comes to Me, and does not hate his own father and mother and wife and children and brothers and sisters, yes, and even his own life, he cannot be My disciple (Luke 14:26).

Christianity is spiritual, but spirituality is not necessarily Christian. Being a spiritual person does not make one a Christian. Nor does pursuing spiritual things under the banner of the Christian church. Human beings in general—even the unsaved—are spiritual because God created them that way. Spirituality is certainly a part of Christianity, but a commitment to spirituality (or spiritual formation, or spiritual growth) indicates nothing about one's trust in the finished work of Jesus Christ. We cannot immediately assume "spiritual" equals "Christian."

> God is spirit, and those who worship Him must worship in spirit and truth (John 4:24).

Humanitarianism is not the chief aim of the church. Currently, a new generation is pushing back against the former isolationist strategies of the suburban church. They point out the lack of compassion we have exhibited over the past 50 years. As a result, much is being made—and rightly so—about the need for humanitarianism and compassion in the church. However, humanitarianism is not the goal of the church. It is a means to the exaltation of the name of Christ through the proclamation of the gospel—which is the aim of the church. God the Father could have easily remedied hunger around the world without putting His Son to death. Jesus himself noted the central purpose of His incarnation and contrasted it with the same misunderstanding about humanitarianism in His own culture.

> Truly, truly, I say to you, you seek Me, not because you saw signs, but because you ate of the loaves and were filled (John 6:26).

Christianity is not about being happy but does result in joy. To reduce the Christian life to the attainment of personal happiness and domestic tranquility is to distort Christianity beyond recognition. In so doing, we blatantly read American ambitions into the Christian faith. This ignores reality. The suffering of this present existence touches everyone. Pain is an undeniable effect of the Fall. The Bible acknowledges suffering as a common human experience, but that conflicts with our naive interpretations of the Christian life.

> Consider it all joy, my brethren, when you encounter various trials, knowing that the testing of your faith produces endurance (James 1:2-3).

You cannot find God's will for your life (in the popular sense) in the Bible. The popular idea that a specific zone of existence is out there

for each Christian and may be discovered through a series of principles extracted from loosely interpreted Bible passages is patently mis-
leading. It is also purely American. It is true, given God's sovereignty
over all things, that God is in control of our lives and specific contexts. But to assume that the aim of the Christian life is to find one's
place of impact by reading Bible verses as if they were tea leaves is the
product of raw American narcissism.

> I urge you, brethren, by the mercies of God, to present
> your bodies a living and holy sacrifice, acceptable to God,
> which is your spiritual service of worship. And do not be
> conformed to this world, but be transformed by the renew-
> ing of your mind, that you may prove what the will of God
> is, that which is good and acceptable and perfect (Romans
> 12:1-2).

Being a Christian is not about being a good person. You do not need
Jesus to be a good person. There are plenty of good people in our
communities who have nothing at all to do with Christ. In reality,
Christianity is about repenting of our confidence in our own goodness and fleeing to the righteous life of Christ.

> There is none righteous, not even one;
> There is none who understands,
> There is none who seeks for God;
> All have turned aside, together they have become
>   useless;
> There is none who does good,
> There is not even one (Romans 3:10-12).

You will not have your best life in this existence. This too is a common suburban Christian theme that has no real basis in Scripture.
Given the presence of sin and its impartial effects, this goal is an
impossibility for many faithful believers. Murder, cancer, crime, tragedy, and the like are all evidence of the earth's desperate need for
redemption. This trite Americanized message ignores the tragic contexts of many around the globe. The best still awaits those who love
and long for Christ.

Then the dust will return to the earth as it was, and the
spirit will return to God who gave it. "Vanity of vanities,"
says the Preacher, "all is vanity!" (Ecclesiastes 12:7-8).

God may not want you to be rich. He may want you to be poor. Poverty may be the context in which God places His children in order to
accomplish His purposes in ways they cannot fully understand. The
false gospel of health and wealth, combined with our own materialistic tendencies in the States, has coalesced into this monumental
misunderstanding. As believers, our treasures are eternal. They are
not temporal.

Listen, my beloved brethren: did not God choose the poor
of this world to be rich in faith and heirs of the kingdom
which He promised to those who love Him? (James 2:5).

Wealth is not a sign of God's favor. The relative prosperity of individual people—which is determined by an all-wise God—indicates
nothing about their eternal state or position before God. To think
otherwise is to deny the Bible's central message of redemption by
grace.

The poor man died and was carried away by the angels to
Abraham's bosom; and the rich man also died and was buried. In Hades he lifted up his eyes, being in torment, and
saw Abraham far away, and Lazarus in his bosom (Luke
16:22-23).

Most contemporary Christian music isn't. Who is being serenaded
by those romantic themes emanating from the contemporary Christian stations? One's lover? Jesus? It's hard to tell, and so this genre
is reduced to the level of inconsequence. This type of music seems
mainly to serve as a cleaner version of secular love ballads. The notable absence of Christ's central achievement in most of the lyrics
makes them less than Christian but slightly more than secular.

But may it never be that I would boast, except in the cross
of our Lord Jesus Christ, through which the world has
been crucified to me, and I to the world (Galatians 6:14).

Moral or affluent people need the gospel just as much as immoral or poor people. We seem to forget that the majority of Jesus's audience was comprised of very decent people. He preached the gospel to the good and bad. We have an arrogant tendency to believe that those who live in a certain part of town, those who exist below a certain economic level, or those who are in a certain part of the world are in greater need of the gospel and more open to it. All are in need. Without the grace of God, none will come to know redemption. The affluent are as desperate as the desperate.

> One of the criminals who were hanged there was hurling abuse at Him, saying, "Are You not the Christ? Save Yourself and us!" (Luke 23:39).

America has never been a Christian nation. Religion, God, Judeo-Christian values, Christians, and freedom of religion are certainly undeniable parts of our heritage as Americans. Many Christians and Christian principles were involved in the founding of this country. But this has never been such a Christian nation that the church in America should aim to recover a lost heritage or seek to reconstruct a forgone utopia. Our citizenship is in heaven. Christianity is not a national religion. Every nation eventually meets its end in the rule of Christ on the earth.

> The kings of the earth and the great men and the commanders and the rich and the strong and every slave and free man hid themselves in the caves and among the rocks of the mountains; and they said to the mountains and to the rocks, "Fall on us and hide us from the presence of Him who sits on the throne, and from the wrath of the Lamb; for the great day of their wrath has come; and who is able to stand?" (Revelation 6:15-17).

Austere living is not a sign of spiritual devotion. The current trend toward asceticism among young American Christians is more a reaction to capitalism than obedience to any particular command of Christ. This movement is a response to much larger socioeconomic circumstances in our society and around the world, and it has spilled over into the church. It has resulted in a rejection of church method-ologies that suited the needs of hard-to-please market-driven Ameri-can Christians. But we cannot assume measures of austerity represent a higher commitment to Jesus. If we do, we reduce devotion to Christ to a series of things to be done. When that happens, we measure god-liness against the devotion of others and not the holiness of God.

> These are matters which have, to be sure, the appearance of wisdom in self-made religion and self-abasement and severe treatment of the body, but are of no value against fleshly indulgence (Colossians 2:23).

Culturally relevant messages are often disconnected from the actual point of the Bible. Our demand for goods and services has resulted in a specific style of biblical instruction that is uniquely American. Ser-mons that offer immediately relevant principles are the product of preachers who choose to meet the demands of finicky consumer-minded parishioners rather than preach the truth. Just as we shop for bargains in our malls, we have come to expect the most applicable messages churches can offer in the least amount of time. This envi-ronment of supply and demand has forced many preachers to com-promise biblical methods of interpretation in order to satisfy those who want truths that relate most directly to them. But the biblical message of the cross goes the opposite direction. It appears irrelevant (foolish) to the unrepentant. Biblical Christianity cares nothing for the comfort level of suburbanites.

> The word of the cross is foolishness to those who are per-ishing, but to us who are being saved it is the power of God (1 Corinthians 1:18).

God did not save you because you have intrinsic value. This common sentiment among American evangelicals is proven illegitimate by the relentlessly unfavorable description of mankind found in the Bible. Salvation in the Christian sense is always described as being in spite of us. Our only contribution to our salvation was the need to be res-cued from the wrath of a holy God.

You were dead in your trespasses and sins, in which you formerly walked according to the course of this world, according to the prince of the power of the air, of the spirit that is now working in the sons of disobedience. Among them we too all formerly lived in the lusts of our flesh, indulging the desires of the flesh and of the mind, and were by nature children of wrath, even as the rest. But God, being rich in mercy, because of His great love with which He loved us, even when we were dead in our transgressions, made us alive together with Christ (by grace you have been saved), and raised us up with Him, and seated us with Him in the heavenly places in Christ Jesus, so that in the ages to come He might show the surpassing riches of His grace in kindness toward us in Christ Jesus (Ephesians 2:1-7).

You are not a better person for having become a Christian. Confessing the name of Christ is an admission of our failure as people. To believe in Christ is to disbelieve any good resides within us. Being Christian does not make us superior to the non-Christians in our culture. On the contrary, it is a public declaration to all those we come in contact with that we are unworthy yet saved by grace.

It is a trustworthy statement, deserving full acceptance, that Christ Jesus came into the world to save sinners, among whom I am foremost of all. Yet for this reason I found mercy, in order that in me as the foremost, Jesus Christ might demonstrate His perfect patience as an example for those who would believe in Him for eternal life (1 Timothy 1:15-16).

You should not pattern your life after Joseph, David, Daniel, or any other biblical character. People are not divine just because they appear in the Bible. They are just as human and fallen as we are. In some cases, their lives are more tragic and disgraceful. In every case, their lives prove the universal need for the life of another—Christ. To bind ourselves to the pattern of their lives or to create a system of principles to live by from their stories is only a respectable form of moralism. To approach the biblical figures in this manner is to miss the real story of the Bible.

> All have sinned and fall short of the glory of God (Romans 3:23).

Church is not where you go to escape the influence of the world. In keeping with Christ's commission, the world should fear the influence of the church. The church's slogan is not "Escape and evade until Jesus returns."

> Go therefore and make disciples of all the nations, baptizing them in the name of the Father and the Son and the Holy Spirit, teaching them to observe all that I commanded you; and lo, I am with you always, even to the end of the age (Matthew 28:19-20).

God does not love you more if you read your Bible and pray. God cannot love you any more or less than He already does in Christ. Bible reading and prayer are means through which the Spirit connects our souls to God's astounding love. They are not conditions of His mercy.

> There is now no condemnation for those who are in Christ Jesus (Romans 8:1).

Sinners (even the worst you can imagine) are not your enemies. Before God, the most immoral people in our societies are no more unworthy than we are. They are not beyond God's love, and they are not a threat to the advancement of the gospel. They are our mission field.

> I say to you who hear, love your enemies, do good to those who hate you, bless those who curse you, pray for those who mistreat you. Whoever hits you on the cheek, offer him the other also; and whoever takes away your coat, do not withhold your shirt from him either (Luke 6:27-29).

A Christian president will not save our country or the world. We should give up this pipe dream if we are ever to depend on Christ and hope solely in Him. The gospel impacts a culture soul by soul, not by the legislation of morality.

God highly exalted Him, and bestowed on Him the name
which is above every name, so that at the name of Jesus
every knee will bow, of those who are in heaven and on
earth and under the earth, and that every tongue will confess that Jesus Christ is Lord, to the glory of God the Father
(Philippians 2:9-11).

*The best thing you can do for morally upright people is assume they are
lost.* To immediately assume someone is regenerated or converted in
order to observe a certain level of decency and decorum is to ignore
what the gospel communicates about humanity—even about the
most civilized people. We cannot assume "good" means "Christian."

When Jesus heard this, He said to him, "One thing you still
lack; sell all that you possess and distribute it to the poor,
and you shall have treasure in heaven; and come, follow
Me" (Luke 18:22).

*Finding your purpose in life is not the most important thing you can
do.* Christians' first priority is to commit their lives to God's glory.
The purpose He may have for them is a matter of His righteous will.
To assume that God's greatest concern is to reveal our purpose in life
is to greatly diminish the person and nature of God as revealed in the
Bible. It also greatly inflates our importance in the eternal scheme
of things. In many instances, such ideas are merely code for discontented suburbanites.

"You shall love the Lord your God with all your heart, and
with all your soul, and with all your mind." This is the great
and foremost commandment (Matthew 22:37-38).

Freedom of religion may not be good for Christianity. The absence
of persecution or cost for bearing the name of Christ usually results
in a complacency among the covenant community.

Only give heed to yourself and keep your soul diligently,
lest you forget the things which your eyes have seen, and
lest they depart from your heart all the days of your life; but

make them known to your sons and your grandsons (Deuteronomy 4:9).

Abortion is not what's wrong with America. Abortion, a vile and
heinous evil that should be opposed at every opportunity by those
who claim the name of Christ, is a symptom of the real problem with
humanity—sin. Abortion is not the root of the problem. We should
keep in mind that Jesus pressed the definition of evil to levels that
condemn us all as murderers.

> The heart is more deceitful than all else
> And is desperately sick;
> Who can understand it? (Jeremiah 17:9).

We'll stop there. All of this raises one essential question explored
in this book: How much of what we have assumed to be Christian
out here in the suburbs actually is? Can we ever really know? What
if much of what we've assumed to be Christian is not even close to
the real thing? What if the majority of our practice is only a unique
blend of American values and vague spirituality sprinkled with Christian verbiage? What if the above list is much longer than we imagine?

As it is, I'm convinced a great deal of what we believe to be Christian in the suburbs actually isn't. This is not a unique dilemma. We
should not be surprised by the challenge presented by cultural assimilation. Christians in every culture struggle to make a proper separation between things cultural and Christian. America is no exception.

Within the American suburbs, countless unsuspecting and well-
intended Christians mistake any number of suburban myths (including those I've listed) for Christianity. On a weekly basis, if not daily,
we miss the point about Jesus. We read books, hear sermons, listen
to music, participate in Bible studies, and attend conferences that
never get around to the particulars of real Christianity. The realities
that distinguish Jesus from every other human who ever walked the
earth and make Him more than an example to follow often go unnoticed. Much of what we assume to be Christian in our everyday experience here in America has no real connection to Christianity at all.

Our popular Christianity in the American suburbs is largely a synthetic version of the real thing.

The true gospel message has gone missing in the suburban church. Our citizenship in heaven has been misplaced by our citizenship in the States. If anything, the heart of our faith is a mere ticker running harmlessly beneath our Christian life. We assume it's there and press on to more relevant matters. We completely misunderstand the Christian life in the process of attempting to live it.

But the gospel is everything. It is the Christian life. It is the central focus of the church. It is not something we occasionally tag onto the end of sermons or tip our hat to in the beginning of our "spiritual journey." Its essential message—Jesus Christ, Lamb of God and risen Savior—is who we are and all that we are about. It is what makes the church the church wherever it happens to be. It is what protects us from the formidable idolatry of the suburbs.

The Before and After

Much of the modern church seems removed from the simplicity of its rustic beginnings. The two scenes often have barely a semblance. If you lay their core messages on top of each other, they don't line up. Simply take the Bible at face value and then look around at what's happening. You'll see it. Something has changed in 2000 years since Jesus rose from the dead. We seem to be living in one of those rumor games in which a fact is passed around a circle from ear to ear until it makes it back around to the original source. By the time Christianity got back around to us, it was completely different from the message that was delivered on the streets of Jerusalem. Our message sounds like a television commercial for some superfluous product. It's more of a marketing strategy than an announcement about God's grace.

Remember the first Christian sermon and how desperate with truth it was? The air of the newborn church was thick with confidence, conviction, and power. Peter, the clumsy and blustery apostle known for misspeaking and being pretentious, found a stump and set off a bomb. When he finished, there was but one unavoidable conclusion—Jesus came to save us from who we are and the resulting consequences.

> Now when they heard this, they were pierced to the heart, and said to Peter and the rest of the apostles, "Brethren, what shall we do?" Peter said to them, "Repent, and each of you be baptized in the name of Jesus Christ for the forgiveness of your sins; and you shall receive the gift of the Holy Spirit. For the promise is for you and your children and for all who are far off, as many as the Lord our God will call to Himself." And with many other words he solemnly testified and kept on exhorting them, saying, "Be saved from this perverse generation!" (Acts 2:37-40).

The way the modern suburban church confronts the culture looks nothing like this. Our message has commercial appeal but is generally unable to address man's real need. Peter's sermon was a warning. He stood on the air hose of his culture until it was gasping for the fresh air of the gospel. Repentance was the logical conclusion of what he proclaimed. The modern church preaches a gospel that is a respecter of persons.

We are so very dissimilar from the first preachers. Some might dismiss my vision as a pipe dream by arguing the inevitability of such slippage. "That was then. This is now. That was a unique moment, and those people had just put the Son of God to death." This is the very disconnect I'm intending to point out. This great divide between their experience and ours is not merely the result of the passing of time. Rather, it's a consequence of our failure to apprehend the gospel. The church is still the church. They were on the streets of the community beseeching the world to bow at the feet of the gracious Lamb of God. Until we identify with those early ambassadors, we'll struggle to be who we are.

Their moment in Jerusalem and our moment in the suburbs are not as far removed as we think. We are that same old mob, albeit well-dressed and affluent. Same Savior. Same sinners. Same need. Same consequences. Same message. Same grace. Same stump. Right now this raw vision of church is buried under layers of confusion that have formed over time and distance. What we have is a strange sub-culture of Christianity complete with its own dialect, products, and vision of life. The present moment is so very strange and so very far removed from our commencement. Modernity has swallowed the church whole and left only the bones behind. Our connection to the gospel mission of the true church can put the meat back on.

And the Forces of Modernity
Shall Not Prevail Against It

All you need to do is step back for a moment and pay attention to what's being said and done within popular Christianity. A gaping divide separates the ancient faith described in the Bible from the church in the suburbs. What's left is a strange alteration. The misrepresentation is beyond prevalent. What is this thing we call Christianity in America? Is it real? Is it what we are supposed to believe? Who really knows? It surrounds us. We are the fish. Believe me when I tell you, whether you see it or not, you're imbibing it on a constant basis. It's right there under your life and worship, passing for authentic Christianity. It's a thousand worn-out clichés.

Consider contemporary Christian radio for a moment. No doubt you've preset a few of your dials to your local contemporary Christian stations. A sad and tattered promotion for churches shows up on the radio in every city in America. We've all heard it. It goes something like this.

> Are you tired of traditional church? Do you feel out of place when you attend? Do the messages make you feel guilty? Are you looking for something positive? Are you looking for messages that are relevant? Are you looking for a place where you can belong? You're not alone in your frustration. Church does not have to be boring. Church does not have to be complicated. Come and join us at the Suburban Church, where you can come as you are. It's a church designed with you in mind. We have six service

times, including two on Saturday night. Or you can stay home and watch in your pajamas.

This stuff is like catnip for suburban evangelical Christians. It drives me crazy. It makes me shout at my steering wheel. Seriously, it's absurd. Unrelenting offers like this make up the bizarre Christian subculture I'm describing. This ad is opposed to a biblical view of the church in every possible way. You should not find it appealing. You should find it offensive. Just think through it.

Consider the logic of removing a sense of conviction from church. It's convoluted. The only way a church can avoid causing feelings of conviction is to avoid the gospel all together. But when you abandon the gospel or tuck it safely away out of sight where it can't offend, you've ceased to be the church. How contrary to biblical reality is plugging a ministry for its accommodation and not its faithfulness to the Christian message? That's sheer consumerism.

Fact is, a person who is drawn into this type of ridiculous marketing strategy is the very person who needs to feel the sting of the cross. He does not need to be made to feel comfortable. He needs to feel needy. After all, until the gospel exposes his real condition and need before God, he'll never come to know the sweet mercy of Christ. Ultimately, you can't find acceptance, mercy, and love in a church that doesn't constantly proclaim the gospel of grace.

Then there's the massive assumption implicit in the overall message—the audience is comprised of Christians who need only to find a church that works for them. That assumption is extremely dangerous. Moral people who drop spiritual and Christian-sounding terminology must surely be Christian. If people gravitate toward spiritual and religious stuff, they must be born again. There's no way to describe how deadly this assumption is or the damage it has already done to the body of Christ. It's the wrong starting point altogether.

Furthermore, what are we to do with the very obvious contradiction found in the criticism of traditional churches? "Those traditional and boring people are judgmental, so come over here with us. We don't do that." This bit of irony kills me. It's basically saying, "We're much better than self-righteous people." How self-righteous is that? We should be insulted by such blatant hypocrisy, not drawn to it.

And the appeal of convenience is totally deceptive. Obviously, churches who design their facilities or present information in a way that is helpful to attendees are not compromising the gospel by doing so. They're using common sense. But to imply that the church exists to accommodate the comfort levels and felt needs of suburbanites is just not true. It's disingenuous. Christianity is the most inconvenient religion known to man. You have to be utterly inconvenienced to be a part of it at all. Death to self. Service to others. After all, Jesus is Lord. He may demand that you do things that result in tremendous discomfort and that are extraordinarily inconvenient. A church built on convenience is not a church. It's a religious spa.

The point is, a message that sidesteps the sting of the cross does not square with the biblical picture. Yet this type of misrepresentation is everywhere. It's in the very fabric of the modern American church. It gets in your head and has you believing things are real when they aren't real at all. It creates a virtually inescapable delusion. We are all influenced by it.

This book is about our need to unplug from the delusion and reconnect with the true gospel heritage of the church of Jesus Christ. We have but one message. There are many brilliant corollaries and effects, but not many messages. Our present challenge is to keep the margins from supplanting the center.

The church is a group of sinners saved by grace who have been drug together by the gravitational force of mercy, the love of Lord Jesus Christ, and the regenerating power of the Holy Spirit. We are a people snatched right out of our stations in life and forced together and onto our knees at the feet of the Lord Jesus Christ. Our parking lots have brand-new European SUVs and '76 Datsuns. The richest person among us is as grateful for the love of God in Christ as a beggar is for a loaf of bread because the richest person is as needy as the poorest. The poorest person among us cannot believe the lavish riches of the grace of God freely received. Therefore the poorest man has as many treasures as the richest. When rich and poor get out of their respective vehicles and enter into the church, they are the same man. Saved by grace.

> He Himself is our peace, who made both groups into one, and broke down the barrier of the dividing wall, by abolishing in His flesh the enmity, which is the Law of commandments contained in ordinances, so that in Himself He might make the two into one new man, thus establishing peace, and might reconcile them both in one body to God through the cross, by it having put to death the enmity. And He came and preached peace to you who were far away, and peace to those who were near; for through Him we both have our access in one Spirit to the Father. So then you are no longer strangers and aliens, but you are fellow citizens with the saints, and are of God's household, having been built on the foundation of the apostles and prophets, Christ Jesus Himself being the corner stone, in whom the whole building, being fitted together, is growing into a holy temple in the Lord, in whom you also are being built together into a dwelling of God in the Spirit (Ephesians 2:14-22).

Church is not about convenience at all. It is about service. It is not about avoiding feelings of guilt. It's about hearing how all our guilt was placed on another. It's about reading all our deserved condemnation into the condemnation of Jesus Christ. It's not about being accepted per se. It's about the wonder of our acceptance before God due to the righteous life and sacrifice of Christ. Neither is it a group of nonconformist hipsters avoiding the stereotype of traditional church. Church transcends a ridiculous notion like this. There are suits and ties. Jeans. Traditionalists. Nontraditionalists. Longtime church people. Unchurched people. It's the church. Church cannot be reinvented and restyled—well, not the real church anyway. The real ad for church should go something like this.

> Is Christ your Lord? Have you been redeemed by His blood? Are you still stunned by the grace of God? Do you

stand in awe of the glory of Christ? Are you a sinner saved by grace who desires to gather with other sinners saved by grace and praise the Lamb who was slain from the foundation of the world? Are you desperate to worship a God who is so gracious and unconditionally loving toward sinners that he would put His only Son to death? Is your heart filled with a desire to share this message of deliverance with everyone you see? Are you looking to lock arms with the redeemed and march out into the city with the gospel of grace and compassion for the lost?

The Greatest Thing Since Sliced Bread

I want to make clear from the beginning that I love the church. This volume is prompted by my love for Christ's bride. At my core I am a churchman. I have been in its trenches for more than twenty years. I believe wholeheartedly that the local church constitutes the merciful God's chief instrument for the evangelization of the world and for His constantly unfolding redemptive mission. Every other useful means we may employ to proclaim the excellencies of the gospel are inferior to the impact and reach of the church. I have given more than half my life to its mission.

As a pastor, simply keeping up with the new strategies to reinvent church or revise ministry is exhausting. There's no end to the approaches and stratagems offered annually by experts in the field of church growth. Lest I be misunderstood, this genre of Christian literature can be beneficial. The information is not worthless. Only small-minded contrarians would think otherwise. Honestly, I've found numerous jewels tucked into the pages of many of these "church in a box" programs. I do read them. At the minimum they can help a pastor see the clutter in his ministry.

But fundamentally, church is not as simple as applying a series of techniques. There are too many variables in a church to follow such a simplistic approach. Ultimately, even the most helpful books and programs end up in used-book stores and yard sales as they are overrun by the passing of time and new challenges. They are based on a lot of presumption (so little of our strategies are the reasons churches succeed or don't) and a limited amount of helpful information. Negatively, they have a tendency to suspend faithful ministers over the bottomless mire of success-driven goals. In too large a dose they are distracting. At the end of the day it's down to a desperate man who is himself desperate for desperate people. Dr. D.A. Carson put it this way.

> At the moment, books are pouring off the presses telling us how to plan for success, how "vision" consists in clearly articulated "ministry goals," how the knowledge of detailed profiles of our communities constitutes the key to successful outreach. I am not for a moment suggesting that there is nothing to be learned from such studies. But after a while one may perhaps be excused for marveling how many churches were planted by Paul and Whitefield and Wesley and Stanway and Judson without enjoying these advantages. Of course all of us need to understand the people to whom we minister, and all of us can benefit from small doses of such literature. But massive doses sooner or later dilute the gospel. Ever so subtly, we start to think that success more critically depends on thoughtful sociological analysis than on the gospel; Barna becomes more important than the Bible. We depend on plans, programs, vision statements—but somewhere along the way we have succumbed to the temptation to displace the foolishness of the cross with the wisdom of strategic planning. Again, I insist, my position is not a thinly veiled plea for obscurantism, for seat-of-the-pants ministry that plans nothing. Rather, I fear that the cross, without ever being disowned, is constantly in danger of being dismissed from the central place it must enjoy, by relatively peripheral insights that take on far too much weight. Whenever the periphery is in danger of displacing the center, we are not far removed from idolatry.[1]

In reality, the church does not need to be rethought, reorganized, reconstituted, reprogrammed, recontextualized, or revised. The innumerable programs that marketers have peddled wear me out. Who are these men who have finally discovered the key to effective ministry? Where have they been? As Carson suggested, how unfortunate they weren't alive in the time of Luther, Whitefield, and Spurgeon. Just think what these great men could have accomplished in the name of Christ if only they had access to the profound demographical statistics of professional church makers.

The church does not need retrofitting. The church needs to be rediscovered. It is buried under our "church in a box" programs. We have sought to make it something it's not. The church needs to be uncovered. It is buried under our arrogant assumption that we can improve on an unbreakable confidence in the gospel and raw desperation for the lost. You cannot program sincerity. Sincerity is a result of understanding the radical implications of grace. That is what the early church had and all truly impactful churches possess.

Back to Basics

At Community Bible Church, where I pastor, we've been bumping up against space issues for the better part of ten years. In ministry circles, we describe this as the kind of problem that beats the alternative. Basically, we attend and worship on top of each other. Honestly, I expected we would have made some sort of facility adjustment by now. But due to a combination of factors, our attempts to find a more suitable space proved unsuccessful. We ran into one obstacle after another. At present all our plans are on hold. In the interim we've gotten along with what we have. Let's just say it's cozy.

We worship in a "fellowship center." Okay, it's a gym. But we choose to refer to it as the sanctinasium. The name helps us feel better. Part gym, part sanctuary. It's a simple structure, an unadorned multiuse facility adjusted to look like the inside of a church on Sunday mornings. After a while, and if you don't look up, you don't even notice the basketball goals hanging from the ceiling. Or the chairs that have to be stacked every Sunday. It's the most used facility on our campus, so it requires a lot of maintenance. It's starting to tatter around the edges. As the one person who stares at all the defects every Sunday, I can't help but notice them. There's a lot of room for improvement. Frankly, the duct-tape effect doesn't help me deal with the dream of a new building. It pesters me like an ecclesiastical new-car smell.

Before, the idea of a new facility dominated my long-term vision for the church. I dreamed (and still do) of what could be done should we ever increase our square footage at a better location and a build-to-suit structure. New ministries. An expanded launching pad for the gospel. New people. Access to different communities. Basketball goals in the right building. Chairs that stay put. Now, while it is a real need (Don't think for a moment I've given up the dream!), the wait has had a profound effect on my vision of church. I may have found the church inside the church while trying to build a church.

As it turns out, we've not really wanted for anything in the mean-time. If anything, making do has helped us get in touch with what really matters. It reminds me of my first year of seminary, when my wife, Robin, and I barely had enough money to live on. Twenty-cent cans of tomato sauce and ramen noodles kept us alive. We had little luxury but experienced an uncluttered and luxurious joy in our lives and marriage. It's amazing how you discover what's important when you discover what you can live without.

This moment in our church is like that moment in my life. For certain, people aren't showing up for the amenities. Or maybe they aren't showing up because of the amenities. Same outcome either way. People attend CBC because of what's inside. Or more specifically, because of who's inside. It's a real gospel community. True fellowship. Real "inreach" and outreach with the gospel. It's an unassuming sort of worship experience. No one is here for a show. Our attitude kind of mirrors our facility. We take the truth seriously but ourselves not so seriously. As it stands now, our greatest concern is not getting to a new facility, but preserving who we are when we do. In a word, the ministry of CBC is simple. Utilitarian at best.

As it turns out, Christians are hungry for simple and basic. Many have been lost in churches designed to protect anonymity, and they are hungry to know and be known by a real community of saints. It's no surprise that we're picking up people from the surrounding evangelical community for this very reason. Obviously, we didn't plan this. This isn't some amazing double reverse psychology of church strategy. Actually, we're the tie that stayed in the closet so long it came back in style. I realize what I am about to say is cliché, but also happens to be true. Churches aren't buildings. Churches need buildings and spaces to function, but churches are not the sum total of their facilities. Churches are people. When you can get (and stay) here, everything else falls into its proper place. You don't forget what matters.

I'm grateful that I've lived as a Christian in the decades I have. So much has happened in my time in the church and ministry. No doubt, history will look back on these years as some of the more transformative the church has ever experienced—for better and for worse. The many forces that have shaped it are never-to-be-repeated features of these unique decades of world history. These are peculiar events. Innumerable transitions have occurred and are occurring.

Gospel-centeredness is the latest influence having an impact on the American church. (That was such an ironic sentence to write.) How far away from the biblical reality have we wandered when focusing on the gospel has become the latest way to do church? Very far indeed, but I'm thankful nonetheless. Books are being written left and right announcing the rediscovery of the gospel of God's grace. The reformers must be rolling their eyes.

We are witnessing the intrusion of the true gospel into modern evangelicalism—a disturbance I heartily welcome. As the emphases of sovereign grace, imputation, justification by faith, and the like wedge their way back into the conscious of the church, they bring a singular focus on the gospel. All of these are part of the greater mosaic of redemption. The more we come to appreciate the core of the gospel, the more people are unplugged from the current delusion of Christianity. I have been and am constantly being unplugged.

But I'll warn you now—waking up is not always a pleasant process. The sense of deception one feels can be very distressing. I myself have been through it. It's like learning later in life that you were adopted as a child. You go looking for your true heritage and wonder how much of your life experience is valid at all. You immediately feel betrayed by everything you know. You have to rediscover the truth. Such is the effect of the gospel.

This book is not specifically about gospel centeredness. That message has been so well articulated by others that any addendum by me would be the equivalent of white noise. Horton, Bridges, Keller, Carson, Tchividjian, Wilson, Chandler, and others have all honed the message for a new generation of believers. They have spread the message of Jesus, Paul, Athanasius, Calvin, Burroughs, Warfield, Machen, and a host of others. I have read their works and thank God for them all. They have each helped reawaken my own soul to the truth of the gospel.

This book is the volume before theirs (although I in no way pretend to be their equal in influence). It's a prologue to the details of redemption they expound so thoroughly in their works. My basic message explains why messages like theirs are so important for suburban Christians to hear.

The Leftovers of Seeker-Sensitive Churches

The seeker movement, which unofficially began back in the 1970s, started with people who were frustrated that the traditional church seemed unable to reach the lost. We critics often forget that the seeker movement has noble beginnings. At its core was a concern for evangelism. As church leaders (who had grown up within traditional church models) noticed that their tradition was unable to connect with the lost, they began to rework their own models of church to be more sensitive and attractive to unbelievers. The seeker model became "church for the unchurched." Church services were designed as places where unbelievers with a bent toward spirituality, or who were genuinely curious about Christianity, could comfortably be exposed to the faith. The church service was designed with the unsaved in mind. The traditional model of church—that the church is primarily for believers—was modified to lean more toward accommodation of the unsaved.

In order to create a culture of seeker sensitivity within the church, several shifts in ministry philosophy and methodology had to take place. First, the church would need to focus on accommodating the presence of unbelievers if it were to reach them. Among other things, this meant that various symbols, doctrines, or traditions that had no meaning with unbelievers, or which could unnecessarily offend, needed to be minimized. Having gospel conversations with the seeker was a stated goal but did not define the content of the services. The unbeliever had no real context for words or concepts like "sin" or "atonement," so they fell out of rotation or were reserved for converted church members in specialized classes. Strangely, the gospel ended up being marginalized.

Second, the church would have to prove that Christianity and the Bible were relevant to the needs and contexts of the suburban unbeliever. Since the seeker is asking, "What's in Christianity for me?" the church's responsibility was to demonstrate the relevance of the Christian faith. Topical messages and sermon series on various relevant issues including marriage, money, parenting, sex, and happiness replaced expositions on the gospel. The seeker movement competed for the attention of unbelievers by combining church-growth marketing techniques with a product that was immediately relevant to their lives. This approach had an especially effective impact on suburbanites whose worldview was dominated by a demand for goods and services. The gospel has become a product.

Third, the church started viewing the gospel primarily as a by-product of effective strategy. The aim of the model was to get the unbeliever in church and then to evangelize him through a more relational environment. Seeker strategists referred to this as "permission marketing." As various obstacles in the mindset of unbelievers are overcome, seekers grant Christians an opportunity to demonstrate the gospel's relevance to their lives. Church as the corporate worship of Christians was replaced by church as the corporate evangelization of the lost. Church was redefined.

Some good has resulted from the seeker movement (such as an emphasis on the lost), but the overall impact has been detrimental. Not discounting the validity of the movement's original concerns, it's hard to estimate how much long-term collateral damage has been caused by its strategies. Almost imperceptibly, after 40 years of thinking through the lens of church marketers, dramatic shifts in the American evangelical culture have taken place. The effect is so pervasive that even those who have never been a part of a seeker-style church have had their understanding of Christianity and the gospel shaped by the seeker philosophy. Most evangelicals have no idea how much this era of evangelicalism has shaped their view of Christianity and the church. It's all around us. The various effects are easily spotted from 30,000 feet.

- Church is less a gathering of the redeemed coming together in gospel communities to focus on the unending relevance of the gospel. It's more a place we go at the beginning of our week for spiritual therapy.

- Church is more about the changed life of the individual and not the greater community of saints.

- The "success" of a church is rarely measured by its stewardship of the gospel and often gauged by its size.

- Generally, people choose churches not by their doctrinal commitments or historic creeds, but according to the church's relevance—in message and ministry—to their private lives.

- Relevance is assumed by most to be the most important aspect of a church.

- The Bible is no longer primarily a message of what God did for sinners in Christ, but a spiritual handbook and decision-making guide based loosely on principles extracted from the exploits of biblical characters.

- Church services are rarely billed as the place the church gathers on Sunday to equip itself for evangelism on Monday. That is, evangelism is viewed less a responsibility of the individual—the redeemed declaring the gospel in their cubicles and cul-de-sacs—and more an overall program of the church.

- Most importantly, the gospel, due to the incessant emphasis on relevant messages, is viewed mainly as a means of personal spiritual fulfillment and not a rescue mission of a gracious God. Ultimately, the suburban gospel is ultimately about God wanting us happy and finding meaning in this life.

The seeker movement is relevant to a discussion about the church in the suburbs—and it's a central concern of this book—because suburbanites were the target audience. Historically, seeker churches are a suburban phenomenon. The seeker movement and the church-growth model were designed with the values and tastes of suburban audiences in mind. Designer Christianity. The question was largely, how do we reach the affluent audiences of the upwardly mobile suburbs? Ultimately, the seeker movement was a mission strategy for reaching finicky suburbanites. Such was the finding of a study conducted by the North American Mission Board in 2002—a study that favored the strategy.

> Therefore these churches tend to find themselves in an upper middle class suburban area where there is a growing population of professionals wanting to connect with God but not in a traditional existing church. If this component is not present, then it becomes harder to have the critical mass necessary to start this church.

The same report went on to identify key traits of those targeted by this ministry model. It's what they referred to as the "Common Demographic Profile."

> upper middle-class
> professional

suburban
Anglo

In other words, it's purely suburban. Generally, seeker models don't succeed in the absence of relative material prosperity and financial security. This is why megachurches are rarely near urban centers. Of the 100 largest churches in America, only a handful are near urban centers. In a strange twist of irony, the seeker model is basically irrelevant in the larger population centers of our country.

I mention all this not because I want to add to the mounds of critiques the seeker movement has already suffered, but because this awareness is central to understanding the challenges of Christianity and ministering the gospel in the suburbs. Much of my task as a pastor out here is correcting the collective distortions about Christianity, the church, and the gospel the seeker and church-growth movements left in their wake. We're very much like those fish—we need to spend some time lying on the deck of a boat. Suburban evangelicals have been swimming in the influence for decades unaware.

In the beginning, the seeker movement set out to reach the unchurched of the suburban mission field. As it receded, it left a mission field comprised mainly of the nominally churched. Although missiologists might criticize me for using such precise language, I would argue that the affluent American suburbs represent some of the greatest unchurched (in the true sense of the word) regions of our country. The presence of so many churches out here means nothing as it concerns the presence of an effective gospel witness.

It's important to understand that my target audience is the Christians wandering aimlessly out in the American suburbs, unaware that they are currently imbibing a designer religion that has no essential relationship to Christianity. I'm writing to soccer moms and white-collar dads. What we count as Christian was made in America. It is not the faith once imported from the streets of Jerusalem. The seeker movement, which reaped its bounty in the materialistic wonderland of the American suburbs over the last several decades, has left a biblically desolate landscape behind it. Those who now wander through its vestiges Sunday after Sunday are unaware of the magnificent truth contained in the true message of the church of Christ—the gospel. Much of what they have been told Christianity has to offer, it doesn't. But what they actually need, it does. My heart hurts for suburbanites. I want them to see it. It is glorious.

I will address four specific areas. First, I will expose and describe the effect of the suburbs on Christianity. I will give you an idea of that which envelops you and excludes a truly Christian view of life. The suburbs have an imperceptible power over Christians.

Second, I will reveal the way we so often assume that people know and have embraced the gospel. My aim is to demonstrate our confusion regarding the very realities that actually constitute Christianity.

Third, I will attempt to deconstruct the mess we've made of the Bible and its core message. The real story is so much better than the one we've invented. I can almost guarantee that the majority of evangelicals are missing the point of the Bible on a regular basis.

Fourth, I hope to lift the clutter off our concept of church. We are so much more than we have come to know. When we see ourselves as we truly are, the church becomes the church indeed.

My prayer is that these four emphases will result in clarity. The aim is to systematically walk us out of the fog of American suburban Christianity and into the bright light of the real thing.

Suburbianity: Lies, Myths, and Suburban Legends

The gospel confronts us with the hopelessness of our sinful condition. But we don't like what we see of ourselves in the gospel, so we shrink back from it. We live in a land of self-improvement. Certainly there are steps we can take to make ourselves better. So we modify what the gospel says about us.

DAVID PLATT

The Pharisees and their scribes began grumbling at His disciples, saying, "Why do you eat and drink with the tax-collectors and sinners?" And Jesus answered and said to them, "It is not those who are well who need a physician, but those who are sick. I have not come to call the righteous but sinners to repentance."

LUKE 5:30-32

Escaping the Vortex of Suburban Christianity

Let's be honest. The desire for personal fulfillment fills many churches and moves the majority of Christian books. This emphasis is an omnipresent tease. It's the life-coach guy disguised as a preacher, a romantic ballad played as a Christian song, and a self-help seminar delivered as a sermon. It's everywhere. It hooks us all. "You too can have an impactful and influential life." "You can do something great." Some authors and pastors come right out and guarantee it. "Do these few things and your life will change." Even when authors go out of their way to stress the fact that it's not about you, they go on for 200 pages to talk about you.

Even if the subject is heaven, it's not exactly about enjoying God's glory and the Lamb who was slain for all eternity. It's about how we can escape our unsatisfactory conditions surrounded by all the pagans here on earth. Even if it is about finding God's will, it's not really about God's will. It's about God recognizing how useful we are to Him. When authors stress the importance of service, it's not really about others. It's about the satisfaction we can get in serving others. When they encourage you to pray, it's not about communion with God, but about satisfying your soul's spiritual itch. Even when they stress community, it's not about a group of people suffering for the sake of the gospel. Rather, it's about you finding a place of significance. Words like "best," "purpose," "authentic," "influence," and "intentional" are deliberate. They're buzzwords for suburban Christians. We eat them up. We love them.

There's good reason. These themes tap into the deep ache from which every human on this planet suffers. A vacancy we all know is there and can't ignore. A growl of our soul we spend our lives trying to satisfy with all the wrong stuff. People. Money. Success. Possessions. Appearances. Sex. But none of this quite fits that space. So we move on to the next thing. We go on wandering the planet not knowing who we really are or what we're supposed to be doing. Our legacy is composed of tasks, routines, the latest TV series, soccer practices, and grocery lists. We're nomadic and homeless. We're empty, so we ache. This is not as God intended. We're meant for so much more. Believe me, there is something that fits that hole in your life. It's out there and you can find it. When you do, you'll know it. It's an encounter destined to change you forever. A point from which you can never return. A benchmark. You are never the same. Just as when Moses wandered into the path of a burning bush, things change. At that moment he found himself and what he was supposed to be. Your burning bush awaits.

See how easy that was? Admit it! You were sucked right into the vortex of the bestseller list. Open mouth and insert hook. You were thinking, "My life is about to change. I'm not settling for mediocre anymore. I'm going to start journaling." I was Billy Mays, and you were about to buy a squeegee you didn't need. Without even realizing it we did a 180 right back to us and our happiness. Deepak Chopra could have written that. He probably has somewhere. There is nothing uniquely Christian about it. It's not Christianity. It's suburbianity.

Suburbianity is the general conviction among professing evangelicals that the primary aim of Christ's death was to provide us with a fulfilled life. We came to this perspective by persistently reading the mindset and aspirations of the suburbs into the biblical story. It relentlessly seeps into our Christianity. It comes through in nearly all forms of Christian media, including songs, books, movies, and sermons. God has big plans for you. You are important. You should not be discontented. There's more out there for you. This is the suburban gospel. By it we've saved countless sinners from a poor self-image but not much else.

This message has been recycled and repackaged so many times it's impossible to count the versions. It's easy to get caught up in it. It's been here from the beginning of time. Satan used it on Eve. You're important. Your happiness is essential. Don't let anything hold you back. Blah! Blah! Blah! The only difference between then and now is that Eve had to be convinced that God didn't want her happiness. Nowadays, we spend all our time convincing people that their happiness is all God wants!

Christianity is not about any of this ridiculous nonsense. In fact, this message is stripping the church of its power. It's not even biblical. You can't find it anywhere in the Bible. You may cite Moses, but he never meant that. Even if you make Jesus say it, He didn't really. Jesus never commissioned anything close to this. We've made all this stuff up.

But someone will object, "God wants us to be happy. Jesus said in John 10:10 that He came to give us life more abundantly." But this is exactly my point. We assume that's what He meant because we read the Bible through the grid of self. Takeaways like this are by-products of a narcissistic hermeneutic. There's no way to read the Gospels or the epistles at face value and come away thinking that Jesus walked this earth delivering a self-improvement seminar. That never happened.

Steeples and Treetops

I live at the epicenter of suburbianity. As I write this, I'm in a coffee shop in the suburbs of Nashville, Tennessee. This town has more steeples than treetops. Round here Christianity comes in the mail. Everyone is a Christian. I'm not even kidding. After all, the Christian publishing and music industries are headquartered here, so how can it not be true? You've no doubt heard Mark Driscoll describe the density of anti-Christian sentiment in Seattle. "More dogs than people." Yeah, well, this is exactly the opposite. It is like living in the Holy Land Experience in Orlando. More Bibles than people. It will corrupt you if you let it. Every once in a while we need to be unplugged from its matrix. Can I please take the red pill?

This city is the capital of pop Christianity. Church services could rightly be called free group therapy. "Three ways to improve such and such." And it doesn't stop on Sunday night. It spills out into the community during the week. Nearly every morning, breakfast shops turn into ad hoc churches. Soccer moms and white-collar dads in their uber-trendy cowboy-cut shirts gather to review the latest "pretty book." Young single men and dads huddle with spiritual mentors. Countless churches are represented. Words like "authentic" and "purpose" rise from the tables like Christian incantations. It's a little eerie.

Outside the boundaries of the South, no one cares if you're a Christian. On the edges of the country, Christianity is a foolishness reserved for the naive. Not so in Nashvegas. It's like stepping into an evangelical biosphere where the mayor is a Sunday school teacher. Where else would a local Starbucks—a brand known for its political correctness—advertise a Christian speaker delivering a lecture on overcoming spiritual insecurities? For $20 you can discover how the crucifixion was designed to set you free from your daddy wounds. You can't make this stuff up. You've got to see it to believe it.

It's fun to watch Christians transplanted from the coasts figure this out. The good-ol'-boy Christianity weirds them out. Their first question is, "How in the world do you evangelize in a town where everyone is saved?" Believe me it is tricky. You inevitably end up offending entire family trees when you do. But the offense is necessary. Good people are hard to evangelize.

Keep in mind I'm from the religiously dense south. Bred and raised. Religion is a pastime down here. Church is in our blood. If someone drops Christian-sounding verbiage, everyone assumes the best. All the people you see are Christians. Just ask them. They were born into Christian homes. They've never cheated on their wives. They've attended Sunday school since they were young. If you ask someone, "Are you a Christian?" he will immediately tell you where he goes to church. It's all one big ongoing assumption.

But biblical Christianity assumes nothing. It conflicts directly with the suburban church. The cross is a vandal down here in our heavily churched neighborhoods, incessantly defacing our facades with embarrassing truths, including "You are not as good as you think you are." The cross is a perfect visual representation of the truth suburbanites spend their lives coverng up. Our real problem— and the source of all our problems in one way or another—is a deep-down wickedness. Not even plastic fish on a minivan will cover this up. The cross is no respecter of zip codes and last names. It offends us. This was the same offense Jesus caused in His own community. Just ask the rich young ruler. The cross communicates the most amazing truth about the grace of God as well as the most horrifying reality of our true condition. We cannot avoid the implication of the cross. Nonetheless, we've done a good job trying.

The cross doesn't sell well. After all, who would center his message around something that so disparages a person's identity and sense of self-worth?

Question: "What's in Christianity for me?"

Answer: "Death and insignificance."

Response: "No thanks."

The cross is foolishness. Obviously, we've figured this out. So we created a completely different need—happiness. And this need just so happens to require a much more appealing solution—fulfillment. I picture Jesus sitting in the pews of our churches listening to our saccharine distortion of the gospel and looking down, confused by the scars on His hands.

> He Himself bore our sins in His body on the cross, so that we might die to sin and live to righteousness; for by His wounds you were healed (1 Peter 2:24).

The manifestations of the suburban gospel border on ridiculous. For example, consider this quote from a Christian book by a popular author.

> Here is the good news: When you flourish, you become more you. You become more that person God had in mind when he thought you up. You don't just become holier. You become you-ier.

"You-ier?" Really? Are we serious? That's cheese straight out of a can. Somehow, in ways I've never quite understood, Jesus supposedly makes us happier by dying a horrifyingly brutal death, naked and beaten and hanging on a cross. Did He really need to die for this to happen? Couldn't He have put on a seminar and charged $20? We've romanticized the cross and moved it to the back quadrant of the local Christian bookstore—over where they sell Testamints and What Would Jesus Do bracelets. I think we know what Jesus would do.

Here's the truth. If you're unhappy and don't know why, it's probably because you're looking to be happy. It's because you've been duped into thinking your life has untapped intrinsic value. I'm not saying you're unimportant. (Okay, maybe I am.) I'm simply pointing out that we're not as important as we want to be or as we've been told we are. Anytime we make it about us we're bound to be miserable.

Strangely, when it comes to Christianity, seeking our happiness usually ends up making us miserable. Tim Keller put it this way:

> Most people spend their lives trying to make their heart's fondest dreams come true. Isn't that what life is all about, "the pursuit of happiness"? We search endlessly for ways to acquire the things we desire, and we are willing to sacrifice much to achieve them. We never imagine that getting our heart's deepest desires might be the worst thing that can ever happen to us...
>
> If we look to some created thing to give us the meaning, hope and happiness that only God himself can give, it will eventually fail to deliver and break our hearts.[1]

As Paul said, "Just look at yourselves. What's there to be happy about?" Well, here's how he actually said it.

> Consider your calling, brethren, that there were not many wise according to the flesh, not many mighty, not many noble; but God has chosen the foolish things of the world to shame the wise, and God has chosen the weak things of the world to shame the things which are strong, and the base things of the world and the despised God has chosen, the things that are not, so that He might nullify the things that are, that no man may boast before God (1 Corinthians 1:26-29).

The brutal honesty of the gospel is too much for some people, so the trend refreshes itself every several years in some new format. But in the light of the cross, the delusion is not sustainable.

What's Wrong with This Scene?

If you'll just step back for a moment and be honest with yourself, you'll realize that much of our Christianity is in no way similar to biblical Christianity. They're not nearly the same. I think we know this deep down. If you read the Bible at face value and compare its message to our messages, you cannot but realize that we've misplaced the heart of our faith—the gospel. Maybe the only similarity is our vocabulary. We do use Christian-sounding terms. But even the terms have morphed over the years and carry less weight than they once did. Words like "redemption" are cliché. On the whole, our version of church is nearly completely dissimilar from the church in the Bible. We are so far removed from who we really are.

As we encounter Jesus in the Gospels, walking beside the sea and calling His disciples to surrender their lives and plans in order to follow Him, we assume this same calling has no bearing on us. That was a faraway land. Those were unique circumstances. After all, I'm a housewife in the suburbs. Or I'm a businessman in a white-collar jungle. I'm simply trying to make it to retirement.

How radical was that season when people actually gave up all they had to be with Jesus? When one encounter with Jesus turned people's lives upside down and they willingly followed Him to a life of self-sacrifice? In our minds, Jesus's demands have softened over the years and with the onset of convenience. Modernity has changed everything.

This conclusion could not be further from the truth. Jesus's call to His disciples is no less binding and extreme today than it ever was. There is a sense in which Christianity, understood rightly, will always feel rustic and frightening. Even in the suburbs. Jesus's call to follow Him goes out today in the suburbs just as it always has. Only now there is so much more to walk away from.

> He summoned the crowd with His disciples, and said to them, "If anyone wishes to come after Me, he must deny himself, and take up his cross and follow Me. For whoever wishes to save his life will lose it; but whoever loses his life for My sake and the gospel's will save it. For what does it profit a man to gain the whole world, and forfeit his soul? For what will a man give in exchange for his soul? For whoever is ashamed of Me and My words in this adulterous and sinful generation, the Son of Man will also be ashamed of

him when He comes in the glory of His Father with the holy angels" (Mark 8:34-38).

This dream we keep selling in the church about happiness on this planet is out of touch with the truth. You will never find it here. Sin has made sure of this. Mankind tossed a Molotov cocktail into paradise a long time ago. The current order of things is creaking and groaning toward an inauspicious end. Something better awaits us.

> The Spirit Himself testifies with our spirit that we are children of God, and if children, heirs also, heirs of God and fellow heirs with Christ, if indeed we suffer with Him so that we may also be glorified with Him.
>
> For I consider that the sufferings of this present time are not worthy to be compared with the glory that is to be revealed to us. For the anxious longing of the creation waits eagerly for the revealing of the sons of God. For the creation was subjected to futility, not willingly, but because of Him who subjected it, in hope that the creation itself also will be set free from its slavery to corruption into the freedom of the glory of the children of God. For we know that the whole creation groans and suffers the pains of childbirth together until now. And not only this, but also we ourselves, having the first fruits of the Spirit, even we ourselves groan within ourselves, waiting eagerly for our adoption as sons, the redemption of our body (Romans 8:16-23).

Christianity is the purest form of realism. It is an eye-opening awareness of the true state of affairs on this planet and the only real remedy. Everything about Christ and His cross is contrary to the message we keep pumping out. Christ is not a motivational speaker or guru. He is a prophet. He was not looking for a purpose. He had a purpose—dying as a substitute for sinners. He was not interested in satisfying our souls. He came to save them. He was not a life coach. He offered up His life for ours. He was not a spiritualist. He is God incarnate, who died to save us from spiritual death.

So also we, while we were children, were held in bondage under the elemental things of the world. But when the fullness of the time came, God sent forth His Son, born of a woman, born under the Law, so that He might redeem those who were under the Law, that we might receive the adoption as sons (Galatians 4:3-5).

Christianity, the real version, is counterintuitive. Life is not the goal of life. Death is. So too are the glory of God and the exaltation of the cross.

If anyone wishes to come after Me, he must deny himself, and take up his cross daily and follow Me. For whoever wishes to save his life will lose it, but whoever loses his life for My sake, he is the one who will save it. For what is a man profited if he gains the whole world, and loses or forfeits himself? For whoever is ashamed of Me and My words, the Son of Man will be ashamed of him when He comes in His glory, and the glory of the Father and of the holy angels (Luke 9:23-26).

Don't misunderstand me. The Christian life includes happiness, but it's a strange kind of happiness. One that makes room for pain, suffering, and insignificance. One that is untouched by this world. If we discover we have inoperable cancer, we look forward to how God will use it to His glory. The cross makes cancer make sense. Happiness isn't found in our possessions either. We don't envy our neighbor's Escalade. We pray he doesn't worship it. Neither is happiness tied to personal success. We're happy to go unnoticed and underutilized. If we never get the credit for anything we do, this only means God gets it. Our smallness brings Him glory. This makes us happy. The cross overshadows us. This is all so counterintuitive. The cross is the "red pill."

Many would object to such a Spartan description of Christianity by countering with clichés. "Christianity is about a relationship." I hear this all the time. I partly agree. But even this is somehow about us. Was Jesus really stripped down naked by a gang of ruthless

Romans who beat Him and ripped His beard out of His face so He could have a friendship with you? Jesus is not our buddy. We were not created because Jesus was a lonely only child. Christ did not save us because He needed a friend. God did not put His Son to death so you could finally experience a fulfilling relationship. It really isn't about us at all. He is Lord, and you are His subject. If that's the relationship you're referring to, then yes, I agree. God created us for His glory. Christ saved us because saving wretches glorified His Father and put His glorious grace on display (Ephesians 1–2). Only humans could take the substitutionary atonement and make it about the opportunity to have coffee with Jesus. Only Nashville could market it. Only Western suburban evangelicals would buy it.

Life in the Christian Biosphere

Life out here in the suburbs does something to a believer's soul. This bubble can convolute any true sense of the Christian life. The distortion is almost unavoidable. The reasons we're drawn to the suburbs conflict with the reasons God drew us to Himself. It's hard to feel any real need for rescue when your residence comes complete with a sense of personal accomplishment. There's no impulse of desperation with all this convenience at our disposal. Everything is set up to serve our every need and whim. We can't help but extend this same idea to our concept of the gospel. It is there for us the way Redbox is. When we need it. Jesus becomes an evidence of our civility (decent people love Jesus) rather than a sacrifice for our rebellion against a holy God (sick people flee to Jesus).

This emphasis is why so much of the Bible's message gets filtered out in the suburbs. It's too offensive. The unstated rule in our nominal churches is subject avoidance. If we must mention the realities hiding on the dark side of the cross, we must repackage them to comply with our general sense of well-being. The idea of universal and total sinfulness grinds against the constant refrain of self-importance that plays on a loop wherever we go. The topic of sin does not fit in polite company.

Probably the most pervasive corruption of our context is our view of people. We live where we do in part to avoid certain sections of town populated by certain types of people. Safety in the suburbs is not necessarily a sin. It's more common sense than anything. I get that. I certainly don't begrudge someone's success or what that success might afford him. That's not the issue. But prejudice is programmed into our psyche. We have an "us and them" frame of reference. Honestly, when we look out our windows at the men picking up our garbage, don't we automatically make a basic moral judgment between them and us? Don't we assume they're less fortunate? Are we not better off for where we live and work? (Do you know your garbage man's name?) Fact is, we're skewed.

Once while my family was stopped at a traffic signal near our home, a man on a Harley Davidson pulled up beside us. He was wearing standard biker gear. Outlaw helmet, wife-beater T-shirt, and tattoos. (I was instantly in midlife crisis mode.) My oldest son (ten at the time) was in the passenger seat. He turned to me and said, "Look, Dad. That man has tattoos. He needs Jesus." My heart sank. That assumption is damning. I immediately realized I had handed down my own self-righteousness to my son. But this is how we are trained to think. Reprogramming ourselves is nearly impossible. The real victims of our unconsidered assumptions are the people driving minivans stopped next to us, people we never notice.

This perspective distorts our understanding of the gospel and clouds our understanding of the Christian faith. We're bred to assume that a certain neighborhood, lifestyle, income, race, criminal record, or vice constitutes a greater need for redemption. The bad people are out there somewhere. We assume that if people look a certain way, they're in greater need of forgiveness than we are. This is a betrayal of the gospel. The Bible is explicit on this point.

> The LORD did not set His love on you nor choose you because you were more in number than any of the peoples, for you were the fewest of all peoples, but because the LORD loved you and kept the oath which He swore to

your forefathers, the LORD brought you out by a mighty
hand and redeemed you from the house of slavery, from
the hand of Pharaoh king of Egypt (Deuteronomy 7:7-8).

This same message runs the length of the Bible. It is no less clear
in the New Testament. If anything, it is more clear. "All have sinned
and fall short of the glory of God, being justified as a gift by His grace
through the redemption which is in Christ Jesus" (Romans 3:23-24).

It is so very hard to see ourselves in the *all* in this passage when so
many people out there are surely far worse.

I Can Get to the Gospel from There

I recently had lunch with a DJ who works at a "gentlemen's club"
here in Nashville. (No, we did not have lunch at the club.) Life's circumstances have placed him down the street from our cozy little
church in the suburbs. On occasion he attends our church. I asked
him to lunch in order to share Christ with him. Believe it or not,
we talked about the doctrine of election. He was confused by this
thorny conundrum. An obvious smoke screen. The doctrine of election with a DJ of a strip club? How awesome is that? I can get to the
gospel from there.

As we chatted, I wondered what he thought the church's message was. I'm guessing something like, "You can be saved from your
lifestyle." But Jesus did not die to save him from his lifestyle. This is
hard to grasp, I know—especially for those who have been raised to
believe an improved lifestyle is the goal of life. But aren't there plenty
of white-collar financiers with squeaky-clean lives who are plummeting toward hell just as quickly as strip-club DJs? Our suburban gospel would tell him, "You can be like us—*better.*" In reality Jesus died
to save him from the thing that makes this man think his lifestyle
is okay. In the same way, Jesus died to save us "good folk" from the
thing that causes us to think our lifestyle makes us better than the DJ.

I also wondered how my congregation—nearly full of white,
heavily churched evangelicals—would react if they knew this guy
was sitting next to them on Sunday. Would they scoot a bit farther

away? Probably. Would they reconsider their relationship? I doubt he'd be invited over for dinner anytime soon. There are serious implications with this reaction, especially as it concerns the gospel. The implicit distinction we make here demolishes the need for the cross. Suburban Christianity is designed to save us from a bad lifestyle and not the wrath of God meted out against our sin. It's a denial of the central theme of the gospel.

> Just as through one man sin entered into the world, and death through sin, and so death spread to all men, because all sinned—for until the Law sin was in the world, but sin is not imputed when there is no law. Nevertheless death reigned from Adam until Moses, even over those who had not sinned in the likeness of the offense of Adam, who is a type of Him who was to come.

> But the free gift is not like the transgression. For if by the transgression of the one the many died, much more did the grace of God and the gift by the grace of the one Man, Jesus Christ, abound to the many (Romans 5:12-15).

The suburban gospel causes us to slide away from certain people. Only the true gospel would cause us to slide toward them. Only the real gospel would cause even the most respectable person among us to wonder why anyone would sit near him at all.

> It is a trustworthy statement, deserving full acceptance, that Christ Jesus came into the world to save sinners, among whom I am foremost of all. Yet for this reason I found mercy, so that in me as the foremost, Jesus Christ might demonstrate His perfect patience as an example for those who would believe in Him for eternal life. Now to the King eternal, immortal, invisible, the only God, be honor and glory forever and ever. Amen (1 Timothy 1:15-17).

Basically, suburban Christians think they've been saved from lesser evils, such as unhappiness, discontentment, and potentially poor life choices. A former DJ, on the other hand, was saved from much more serious sins. "Praise God for him. How miraculous that God could save someone from that background." This is so wrong.

Truth is, you are just as vile as the worst person you can imagine. Maybe we're more vile, given that we still see ourselves as slightly better than most. The gospel of the suburbs forces this type of distinction in our minds. There are really bad people, and then there are good folk who only need some guidance. That's a false gospel. As far as the cross is concerned, every last one of us was saved off the pole.

> What then? Are we better than they? Not at all; for we have already charged that both Jews and Greeks are all under sin; as it is written,
>
> "There is none righteous, not even one;
> There is none who understands,
> There is none who seeks for God;
> All have turned aside, together they have become useless;
> There is none who does good,
> There is not even one" (Romans 3:9-12).

If you can look up at your bookshelf and trace the last ten years of your Christian life by the various trends in Christian-living publications, you've been had. Hook, line, and sinker. At worst, you've trusted in the wrong gospel. At the least, you've wasted a decade believing the wrong thing about God, Christ, the Holy Spirit, and the church. I'm writing to offer an alternative.

So from the very beginning, it is about God's grace. That never changes regardless of how we may try to repackage it. When Jesus commissioned His church, He did not send us out on the self-improvement speaking circuit. He sent us out to deliver the actual good news to those made weary by self-improvement. He came to save those who are sick, not those who were improving.

The New Asceticism and Investment Bankers

This is secondhand information, but I hear David Platt is the real deal. I have every reason to believe it. I've interacted with numerous people close to David, and they all say the same thing. He lives what he preaches. Given the tendency for trendsetting pastors to bear a likeness to Tony Robbins, this independently verifiable fact is refreshing. What he's written is what he believes. What he believes is what he lives. I'm happy to spread the rumor.

Case in point. Recently, I was seated at the table with a former elder of Brook Hills at a ministry dinner. In the midst of our conversation he reinforced the legend of Platt's sincerity. According to him, at the height of the success of David's book *Radical*—for which he receives no proceeds—David's family downsized. He went from 1900 square feet to about 900. For most Americans, that would be...well, radical. Honestly, I was convicted.

Having recently read Platt's follow-up book, *Radical Together*, I innocently mentioned to this former elder that David had proposed selling the multimillion-dollar Brook Hills facility—which would be consistent with his message. The distinguished gentleman, who had not read the book, nearly choked on his couscous. Apparently, spiritual austerity has its limits.

Books like *Radical* and Francis Chan's *Crazy Love* have struck a chord with recession-conscious Christians. The accoutrements of the church-growth movement are now unthinkable in light of the economic hardships, vast needs, and suffering around the world. More than one modern-day prophet has declared the end of the megachurch era. For young evangelicals, these behemoths of old are what gas-guzzling SUVs are to environmentalists—irresponsible and inefficient. Around church boards, words like "sustainable" are slowly replacing words like "strategic." The small church is now the wave of the future. Rustic is the new relevant.

This emphasis is resonating with individuals on deep levels. I get where they are coming from. Suburbianity has failed them. Downsizing is a new fruit of the Spirit. People are going small. Young rat-race-weary suburban Christians are taking their cues from the likes of Chan and Platt. Reducing square footage. Quitting their corporate jobs. Going overseas. Adopting orphans from all over the world.

Cutting back to one car. Venturing into microfinance. Owning humanitarian convictions. Doing their part to meet needs in their immediate communities. Moving out of their well-to-do neighborhoods. Relocating to the inner city and lower-income areas. All of this, in one way or another, is a reaction against the "what's in it for me" deluge of the past.

Much good has resulted from this shift in thinking. A resurgence of mission mindedness in evangelical pews. Community-conscious Christians. Intimate fellowship. Deep-seated compassion for suffering around the globe. Sincere concern for the less fortunate. Multiethnic congregations. Simplification of church. A return to core convictions. I've seen many of these positive effects in the church where I pastor. Cheesy PowerPoint presentations and sermon props are slowly being replaced by gut-check calls to life examination. "Eight Ways to Better Living" is slowly being replaced by "Eight Signs the Church Is Narcissistic."

Many Christians are now migrating out of the suburban promised land settled by their pragmatic forefathers. There's a reason Rick Warren didn't plant his church in south Chicago. Growth rates in US cities —otherwise known as going where God is working—led him to Orange County. After all, church growth and the inner city are innately at odds. But things have changed. It's no longer about numbers. It's about being genuine and simple. Small churches are popping up in urban areas targeting specific neighborhoods with the gospel. Famously, Francis Chan, who planted Cornerstone in the suburbs of Simi Valley, west of Los Angeles, resigned as its lead pastor. He's headed to the austere realities of inner San Francisco, a place where people desperately need the gospel. The suburbs are the new burned-over district.

It's been interesting watching all this take place in evangelicalism. Some people's commitment to the new asceticism is intense. Affluence is now a veritable unpardonable sin. Similarly, when American Christians travel to third-world countries on short-term mission trips, they often come back disgusted at most Americans' attitude toward prosperity. Two weeks spent boiling your own drinking water has a way of helping you count your blessings.

Even with all the good that has come from this, I do have a few concerns. I pray all this isn't some trend in which middle-class sub-urban Christians have mistaken a desire for spiritual austerity and simplicity with a call to missions. And much more importantly, I'm afraid we may be misunderstanding the gospel. It's the suburban influence that makes us think that people in inner city or third-world areas are in much greater need of the gospel. Maybe we think they are more willing to believe because of their economic situations. But you can't think this way and remain faithful to Christ's message. Further-more, you can't assume people are less needy of the gospel if a church happens to be on every corner. Chances are they've never actually heard the gospel.

I tell our own short-term missionaries, "If you can't weep for the American businessman the way you do for the Haitian, you aren't ready to go to Haiti." If we assume that the disadvantaged in our inner cities (or in third-world countries) need the gospel more des-perately than the privileged on their boundaries, we have indeed mis-understood some things. For certain, we deny man's real need and judge by externals only.

The upper middle classes of the suburbs still need the gospel. Desperately, in fact. As I mentioned, I pastor a suburban church in Nashville. It was once a rural congregation. It's been at its present location for nearly 50 years. About 25 years ago the suburbs overran it. Now there are churches everywhere. A few years back there were 14 church plants in the Nashville metropolitan area. "Like a hole in the head" comes to mind. Why plant churches when there are so many churches already here? Because church planting is a semi-professional sport in this Southern city. I don't mean to demean the efforts of church planters, but planting churches in the bedroom community of Nashville is almost too easy. People do church here. Anyone can plant a church. Even a local weather anchor planted a church here. The logic is not too dissimilar from starting a boy band.

Frosted tips, catchy lyrics, choreography…and you've got a hit on your hands. This place is more religious than Vatican City. If you build it they will come.

But despite the concentration of churches, many of the people who attend have not heard the gospel. The true gospel, that is. The one that has Christ's substitutionary atoning death for sinful men at its core. The one that has reconciliation to a holy God as its high point and every point in between. The strategy of the seeker movement over the past 40 years—which focused on the felt needs of suburbanites—may have spared some from a lack of contentment, but it may not have spared them from the wrath of God.

The fields out here are amazingly manicured, but they are also white unto harvest. I would argue that the most densely churched spots in this country are in the greatest need of evangelism.

There is an amazing opportunity to step into this void with Christ. A revival is taking place among the comfortable. The simple gospel, which we assume resonates only in lower-income contexts, is now also resonating with the overly churched in affluent contexts. After all, it applies to both equally. The gospel has no boundary to contain it. It penetrates all strata of people and society.

So who's going to reach the affluent with the gospel? Who's going to bravely venture out into the wilderness of capitalism and reach those who have been trapped by its power? Who believes the gospel is powerful enough to do this? Who's going to trek out into religiously dense suburbs and stop assuming that the people who look the best have embraced the gospel? The church still needs successful businessmen and wealthy executives who can infiltrate the upper echelons of the corporate world with the good news of Christ. We need investment bankers who can speak deliverance into the context of greed and salesmen whose business trips look more like mission trips. The church needs missional soccer moms.

Heroin Addicts, Homeschool Kids, and Grace

The baptism services at Community Bible Church are gospel

spectacles—very public and very loud declarations of Christ's redemptive work in the lives of sinners. We're trying desperately to get back to the book of Acts, when baptism was viewed as radical and not perfunctory. By design, it's a rather nerve-racking moment for the baptism participants themselves. The edge on these services is an attempt to recover a sense of the real aim and purpose of baptism. I can only imagine how compelling baptism services were in the early days of the church. What kind of stir do you imagine the proselyte immersion of 3000 converted Jews caused in Jerusalem? Do you suppose they understood the implications of what they were doing and saying? I think so.

As I mentioned, at Community we worship in a "sanctinasium"—that's one part sanctuary and one part gymnasium. As a result, we're forced to use a portable baptistery. Basically, it's a rectangular hot tub of religious proportions. But far from detracting from the moment, this clumsy element adds substantial authenticity to it. It helps everyone "get it." This is not a mechanical moment.

The redeemed stand in lukewarm water just a few feet from their brethren, their family members, and unbelievers who have been invited to watch this bizarre Christian ritual. From this watery platform they declare the gospel of Jesus Christ and its application to their lives. Everyone sings the same song. HIV-infected former homosexuals, promiscuous party girls, angry men, drug addicts, porn addicts, exotic dancers, adulterers and adulteresses…they have all made public declarations of their repentance and dependence on Christ's righteousness. The effect on our church is utterly amazing. We really fellowship. We really sing. We really weep. We really rejoice. We really pray. We really love. We really serve. Hands down these are the best sermons of the year.

Once, leading up to one of these amazing services, a young baptism prospect from a Christian family approached his dad and said, "I don't think I can be baptized." When the father asked why, the young man answered, "I don't have one of those stories." You know the kind of story he means, right? The train wreck of a life saved off the street with needle in his arm when a Gideon Bible fell out of the sky and landed on his head and opened to John 3:16. You know...the "I can't believe that person was saved (good for him)" miraculous story. Having sat through some of our baptism services, this young man wondered what he would say. His story was too ordinary. He was a really good homeschool kid. So he opted out.

When his dad informed me of his decision, I was broken. My first thoughts were, "What have I done? Is that the gospel I have preached? Is that what this kid has heard me say? Have I preached a moralistic message that is strictly about the reformation of a lifestyle? Does my gospel apply only to bad people who need to become good ones?" I delivered a sermon at the same baptism service entitled, "What you might have heard me say." The aim was to apologize for losing sight of the message and to recover the biblical gospel. I've been preaching the same sermon ever since. When good suburban folks repent, it's a miracle.

"By grace you have been saved through faith; and that not of yourselves, it is the gift of God; not as a result of works, that no one should boast" (Ephesians 2:8-9).

 **Part 1**

The Gospel

Jesus—the crucified and risen Lord—gets lost in the suburban church. We set Him down in a corner under stacks of religious odds and ends and forget to notice Him. We misplace the need to need Him. Out of heart, out of mind. We confuse "spiritual" with "Christian." Eventually we attend church rather than gather with the redeemed and celebrate the incomparable glory of God in the cross of Christ. So many of us have forgotten the real reason we're showing up week after week. What exactly are we doing? Is this modern version of church actually what we are called to do? How much of these realities we collectively call Christianity actually are? Is this life we live for Christ really about attaining some sort of domestic equilibrium? Where is Jesus in all this stuff we call church? I'm no longer assuming we know.

The Truth Hiding in the Wide Open

The new gospel conspicuously fails to produce deep reverence, deep repentance, deep humility, a spirit of worship, a concern for church. Why? We would suggest that the reason lies in its own character and content. It fails to make men God-centered in their thoughts and God-fearing in their hearts because this is not primarily what it is trying to do. One way of stating the difference between it and the old gospel is to say that it is too exclusively concerned to be "helpful" to man—to bring peace, comfort, happiness, satisfaction—and too little concerned to glorify God. The old gospel was "helpful" too—more so, indeed, than is the new—but (so to speak) incidentally, for its first concern was always to give glory to God. It was always essentially a proclamation of Divine sovereignty in mercy and judgment, a summons to bow down and worship the mighty Lord on whom man depends for all good, both in nature and grace. Its center of reference was unambiguously God.

J.I. Packer

After there had been much debate, Peter stood up and said to them, "Brethren, you know that in the early days God made a choice among you, that by my mouth the Gentiles would hear the word of the gospel and believe. And God, who knows the heart, testified to them giving them the Holy Spirit, just as He also did to us; and He made no distinction between us and them, cleansing

their hearts by faith. Now therefore why do you put God
to the test by placing upon the neck of the disciples a
yoke which neither our fathers nor we have been able to
bear? But we believe that we are saved through the grace
of the Lord Jesus, in the same way as they also are."

ACTS 15:7-11

Joe Knows

It was a typical Sunday. The specific date and sermon escape me, but I'll never forget the encounter afterward. A man who had never attended our church approached me to leave a comment in the ever-present post-sermon suggestion box preachers wear on their souls. I assumed it was going to be a compliment. What preacher doesn't hope against hope? Right? It was not a compliment.

"Hi. I'm Joe. I'm a visitor here this morning. I'm in Nashville visiting my parents over the weekend. They're unbelievers. They don't really get my faith, but out of courtesy to their only son they agreed to attend church with me."

"That's great. Thanks for joining us here at Community."

"Well actually, it's been a huge mistake. I'm sorry I brought my parents here. You've reinforced every stereotype they have about Christianity. I can't believe you preached for forty-five minutes and never mentioned the gospel. This is tragic."

With that he turned and walked away. I was not even given the courtesy of explaining myself. Honestly, I'm not sure I could have formulated an adequate response in that moment. He was several paces away before I actually processed what he'd said.

My initial reaction was to dismiss him as one of those frustrated preacher types who occasionally snipe sermons. Those guys always feel the need to explain how they would say what I said, only differently. I love that guy, only not really. But Joe wasn't angry like one of those guys. He seemed genuinely saddened by the experience. He did not storm off as much as he slumped off.

For a moment I thought it possible he didn't get our style of church. Maybe he was expecting a specific type of gospel invitation at the end of the service. People have come to anticipate them around these parts. Our particular stripe of church does not practice altar calls. But this is not what he meant because this is not what he said.

The effect of his observation was like a gun going off beside my life and ministry. I was stunned. Later, as I struggled with the implications ringing in my heart, I succumbed to the realization that he was right. Maybe on a level deeper than either of us initially understood. For certain, on that Sunday there was no gospel to be found. Not anywhere—beginning, middle, or end. It was a gospel-less church service in a Bible-believing church. The Scripture, singing, prayers, and all the appropriate church apparatus were present, but not the gospel. This is when I saw it for the first time.

Had he been there on another Sunday it's very possible a "gospel appeal" would have been tagged onto the end of the sermon in case any unbelievers happened to be present. I did this very thing on occasion. But it was more than poor timing. It really was tragic. Joe's parents weren't the only ones I had neglected to expose to Christ's love for sinners. My own soul and the people I dearly loved also suffered as a result. And it wasn't just this particular Sunday. It had been countless Sundays. This awareness caved in on me. For years, I had assumed that everyone knew the gospel. I had assumed all these very decent-looking suburbanites gathering together Sunday after Sunday got it. Why else would they be in church?

You might be inclined to defend me against Joe. After all, what can you learn about a church from a single visit? But it's best not to defend me. You can't. Believe me, I've tried. Besides, deep down you're probably trying to get yourself off the same hook. But for the sake of argument, let's say you could speak on my behalf. I can almost guess what you'd say.

"We're all Christians here. We understand the gospel. After all, this is church. We don't need to have it rearticulated or explicitly stated

every Sunday. We get it. We've already believed it. We're not reviv-
alists. We're here growing as believers being equipped to live godly
lives and evangelize the lost. Every sermon does not have to be about
the gospel."

See, I told you not to do that. You've only reinforced Joe's point.
Right now Joe is somewhere saying, "I told you so." And from where
I now stand, I couldn't disagree with you more. If it were possible to
track Joe down, I would not defend myself—I'd thank him. God
used that moment to radically alter my life and ministry. A brief
moment with a visiting churchgoer exposed a gaping hole in my
ministry—a hole the size and shape of a cross. Right then and there I
determined I'd never again assume that my listeners had received the
gospel. Especially here in the suburbs. Joe's my hero. He now lurks
somewhere in every group where I have the privilege of preaching
Christ.

In a real sense, I discovered the gospel hiding in the wide open
of my life and ministry. I feel like one of those unbelievably fortunate disciples on the road to Emmaus who happened upon Jesus as
He was conducting a private seminar on the most obvious fact of the
Bible: It's about Jesus. Those two guys had tons of biblical data and
spiritual speech accumulated over years of religious activity but no
idea what to do with it. This is us. The eye-opening reality of Jesus
drew them together into a process of discovery that would never end.

> He said to them, "O foolish men and slow of heart to
> believe in all that the prophets have spoken! Was it not
> necessary for the Christ to suffer these things and to enter
> into His glory?" Then beginning with Moses and with all
> the prophets, He explained to them the things concerning
> Himself in all the Scriptures...
>
> When He had reclined at the table with them, He took the
> bread and blessed it, and breaking it, He began giving it
> to them. Then their eyes were opened and they recognized
> Him; and He vanished from their sight. They said to one
> another, "Were not our hearts burning within us while He

was speaking to us on the road, while He was explaining
the Scriptures to us?" (Luke 24:25-27,30-32).

And their hearts burned within them. I get that. Jesus ambushed
me too. Once I realized what was missing, my heart burned. I felt as
if I had never read the Bible before. I was constantly happening upon
some new and incredible dimension of the gospel. Once you see it, it
owns you. God's love is so complete and immovable. Seriously, I can
scarcely believe He loves me, but I believe it nonetheless.

Now as I sit down and prepare to preach, I'm no longer preparing to preach as much as I am preparing to be devastated by this solitary idea of sovereign grace. The onslaught of awareness pouring out
of the cross has transformed all elements of my life, ministry, and
church. I am not the same man I was before. I repent from deeper
places than I did before (and over the right things). I obey for better reasons than I did before (and do the right things). I preach with
freedom I never had before (and about one central thing). I'm never
again assuming that any of us understand the gospel. It's way too
obvious to me now. Or so I pray.

Once you become aware of the hole where the gospel goes, it's all
you see. When the toothpaste is out of the tube, it does not go back
in. The awareness is a point of no return. You can't help but notice its
absence. It's missing in the songs we sing. It's missing in the books we
read. It's missing in the messages we hear. The assumption that everyone gets the gospel is rampant in the suburbs.

I would have you know from the outset it's my goal to ruin you
the way Joe ruined me. I want you to notice what's missing, and I
want it to annoy you. It's one of those "don't think about pink ele-
phants" head games. I want you to think you're crazy because you
begin to see the vacancy everywhere. But you're not crazy. The hole
where the gospel goes *is* everywhere. This entire book is aimed at your
ruination. I'm earnestly praying that an assumed gospel would cause
a riot in your soul. When you listen to Christian songs or read Christian books or listen to sermons, I want a question to nag you. "When
will they get to what God has done?"

The Good News

The good news, the gospel, is a declaration of what God has accomplished in Christ for sinners. It is comprised of the set of historic facts surrounding the righteous incarnate life, innocent death, and resurrection of the person Jesus Christ. It is the declaration that this Jesus is the Son of God (God incarnate), who came to earth in order to willingly offer His life as a substitutionary sacrifice in the place of sinners to atone for our sin and its tragic consequences before a holy God. Peter declared this very message in the first sermon preached after the ascension.

> "And it shall be, that everyone who calls on the name of the Lord shall be saved."

> Men of Israel, listen to these words: Jesus the Nazarene, a man attested to you by God with miracles and wonders and signs which God performed through Him in your midst, just as you yourselves know—this Man, delivered over by the predetermined plan and foreknowledge of God, you nailed to a cross by the hands of godless men and put Him to death. But God raised Him up again, putting an end to the agony of death, since it was impossible for Him to be held in its power (Acts 2:21-24).

In short, on the cross Jesus died in the sinner's place, saving us from the consequence of God's wrath and righteous judgment. Jesus fulfilled what were mere shadows contained in the Old Testament Law. He lifted the burden off of humanity and this planet. He lived the life we were incapable of living. He died the death we deserved. He was the perfect, final, and ultimate substitute, sent to remove the burden of the Law from our shoulders. "Christ also died for sins once for all, the just for the unjust, so that He might bring us to God, having been put to death in the flesh, but made alive in the spirit" (1 Peter 3:18).

He substituted Himself for us. When John the Baptist beheld Him he declared, "Behold, the Lamb of God who takes away the sin of the world!" (John 1:29).

His righteousness was imputed to our account. Our sin was laid on Him.

> Surely our griefs He Himself bore,
> And our sorrows He carried;
> Yet we ourselves esteemed Him stricken,
> Smitten of God, and afflicted.
> But He was pierced through for our transgressions,
> He was crushed for our iniquities;
> The chastening for our well-being fell upon Him,
> And by His scourging we are healed.
> All of us like sheep have gone astray,
> Each of us has turned to his own way;
> But the LORD has caused the iniquity of us all
> To fall on Him (Isaiah 53:4-6).

By Jesus's life, death, and resurrection, sinful men can be reconciled to a holy God through faith. The gospel is primarily the objective reality that God saves sinners in the death of His only Son. The holy Father accepted Jesus's offering for sin, as evidenced in the resurrection. "...He who was delivered up because of our transgressions, and was raised because of our justification" (Romans 4:25).

Consequently, those who trust by faith in the righteous offering of Christ by the grace of God (that His life was offered for them) are now saved. "If you confess with your mouth Jesus as Lord, and believe in your heart that God raised Him from the dead, you will be saved" (Romans 10:9).

But redemption encompasses more than the salvation of the individual sinner. It includes all of creation. All that we know and presently behold on this planet will be healed of the destruction we caused.

> Each in his own order: Christ the first fruits, after that those who are Christ's at His coming, then comes the end, when He delivers up the kingdom to the God and Father, when He has abolished all rule and all authority and power. For "He must reign until He has put all His enemies under His feet." The last enemy that will be abolished is death.

For He has put all things in subjection under His feet. But when He says, "All things are put in subjection," it is evident that He is excepted who put all things in subjection to Him. When all things are subjected to Him, then the Son Himself also will be subjected to the One who subjected all things to Him, so that God may be all in all (1 Corinthians 15:23-28).

The believer and the church are parts of a vast movement of God's redeeming power. We are slowly being drug back to Eden and perfection by the perfect obedience of the second Adam. Righteousness, justice, order, and peace will abound by the power of the Lord Jesus Christ's work. All things will be made right. Jesus has done all this.

A Man on Fire

Tragically, Jesus—the crucified and risen Lord—gets lost in the suburban church. We set Him down in a corner under stacks of religious odds and ends and forget to notice Him. We misplace the need to need Him. Out of heart, out of mind. We confuse "spiritual" with "Christian." Eventually we attend church rather than gather with the redeemed and celebrate the incomparable glory of God in the cross of Christ. So many of us have forgotten the real reason we're showing up week after week. What exactly are we doing? Is this modern version of church actually what we are called to do? How much of these realities we collectively call Christianity actually are? Is this life we live for Christ really about attaining some sort of domestic equilibrium? Where is Jesus in all this stuff we call church? I'm no longer assuming we know.

Here's what I can be sure of—the grace of God toward sinners is astounding. An obvious understatement. Every attempt to explain the epoch of redemption ends in another obvious understatement. None of us can get our minds around it—not even the biblical authors, not even angels, not we ourselves when we get to heaven. We will never fully grasp what has happened. We will be standing in heaven one day shaking our head and asking ourselves, "How could

God save me?" God's redemption of sinners is unendingly spectacular. You cannot get to the bottom of it. The Christian life is spent digging up its treasures. If you are comfortable around it, something is wrong with your soul.

The modern church seems to have lost its sense of wonder in the presence of grace. (My own battles this same slippage.) Where is the celebration of what God has done in Christ that was present in the church 2000 years ago? And by "celebration" I don't merely mean worshipping by singing at the beginning and end of our services. I mean, where in our communities of faith is the permeating sense of wonder and joy in the light of what God has done? Where is that permanent smile on the hearts of those who have come to know the love of God? How is it even possible for those rescued by such astounding grace to take it for granted? How can we simply pass by the wonder at the top of Calvary and descend the other side to more relevant matters of "Christian living"? What's happened to us? Maybe out here where crime rates are low and people are remarkably normal, it's hard to maintain any sense of needing rescue. Something is inherently wrong with this. The suburbs have messed with our minds.

Years into his ministry, having put out one fire after another in the church (all tied to the gospel), Paul sat down in a moment of repose while in prison and penned a letter to a group of churches in Asia. We know it as Ephesians. After all those years, having dealt with the details of the gospel on a daily basis and suffered so greatly for proclaiming its core message of salvation by grace, Paul might have moved on to other topics. Something besides grace maybe, some secondary topic of Christianity. After countless scars (both physical and emotional), what came pouring out of the rickety old apostle was a hymn of praise. The reality still owned Paul.

> Grace to you and peace from God our Father and the Lord Jesus Christ.
>
> Blessed be the God and Father of our Lord Jesus Christ, who has blessed us with every spiritual blessing in the heavenly places in Christ, just as He chose us in Him before

the foundation of the world, that we should be holy and blameless before Him. In love He predestined us to adoption as sons through Jesus Christ to Himself, according to the kind intention of His will, to the praise of the glory of His grace, which He freely bestowed on us in the Beloved. In Him we have redemption through His blood, the forgiveness of our trespasses, according to the riches of His grace which He lavished on us. In all wisdom and insight He made known to us the mystery of His will, according to His kind intention which He purposed in Him with a view to an administration suitable to the fullness of the times, that is, the summing up of all things in Christ, things in the heavens and things on the earth. In Him also we have obtained an inheritance, having been predestined according to His purpose who works all things after the counsel of His will, to the end that we who were the first to hope in Christ would be to the praise of His glory. In Him, you also, after listening to the message of truth, the gospel of your salvation—having also believed, you were sealed in Him with the Holy Spirit of promise, who is given as a pledge of our inheritance, with a view to the redemption of God's own possession, to the praise of His glory (Ephesians 1:2-14).

As is clear from this passage, once Paul went up he never came down. This hymn is a masterpiece of redemptive history from eternity to now. Honestly, I'm not sure I fully understand everything Paul says in this chorus of praise. It's a little beyond me. For example, "With a view to an administration suitable to the fullness of the times, that is, the summing up of all things in Christ, things in the heavens and things upon the earth…" What does that mean? I don't fully know.

Paul goes places I've never been and turns corners of transcendence that leave me struggling to keep up. What is clear to me, however, is that Paul never got over the grace of God. If you sat down with him at any stage of his life and ministry, redemption's mystery is what you would hear. He was a scratched record. First and foremost, Paul was a man who never assumed people understood and experienced the gospel of Christ, and he refused to let others make that assumption. His life was dedicated to pointing out the hole in our message. He never backed off of it one single solitary moment. He knew he couldn't. He was immovable. He was a man on fire.

> It was because of the false brethren secretly brought in, who had sneaked in to spy out our liberty which we have in Christ Jesus, in order to bring us into bondage. But we did not yield in subjection to them for even an hour, so that the truth of the gospel might remain with you (Galatians 2:4-5).

Not assuming that people know and have embraced the gospel is a constant struggle. Taking this for granted is our primary plight in the suburban church. We naturally drift away from the thrust of the gospel and toward more popular, traditional, or practical things. "Salvation" becomes another threadbare religious word. We come to church for all kinds of reasons but not the central one. The apostle Paul knew we'd get here.

> I am amazed that you are so quickly deserting Him who called you by the grace of Christ, for a different gospel; which is really not another; only there are some who are disturbing you and want to distort the gospel of Christ. But even though we, or an angel from heaven, should preach to you a gospel contrary to what we have preached to you, he is to be accursed. As we have said before, so I say again now, if any man is preaching to you a gospel contrary to what you received, he is to be accursed! (Galatians 1:6-9).

> I am jealous for you with a godly jealousy; for I betrothed you to one husband, so that to Christ I might present you as a pure virgin. But I am afraid that, as the serpent deceived Eve by his craftiness, your minds will be led astray from the simplicity and purity of devotion to Christ (2 Corinthians 11:2-3).

He was duty bound to deliver one message.

> If I preach the gospel, I have nothing to boast of, for I am under compulsion; for woe is me if I do not preach the gospel. For if I do this voluntarily, I have a reward; but if against my will, I have a stewardship entrusted to me. What then is my reward? That, when I preach the gospel, I may offer the gospel without charge, so as not to make full use of my right in the gospel.
>
> For though I am free from all men, I have made myself a slave to all, that I might win more (1 Corinthians 9:16-19).

Paul's entire ministry was dedicated to one singular thought—God saves sinners by grace through faith in the finished work of the risen Lord, and He is bringing all things to a glorious end. For this formerly self-righteous Jew, this blew him off his high horse and put him on his knees. It was all he had. It was all he wanted. It's all any of us have.

> Whatever things were gain to me, those things I have counted as loss for the sake of Christ. More than that, I count all things to be loss in view of the surpassing value of knowing Christ Jesus my Lord, for whom I have suffered the loss of all things, and count them but rubbish in order that I may gain Christ, and may be found in Him, not having a righteousness of my own derived from the Law, but that which is through faith in Christ, the righteousness which comes from God on the basis of faith, that I may know Him and the power of His resurrection and the fellowship of His sufferings, being conformed to His death; in order that I may attain to the resurrection from the dead (Philippians 3:7-11).

Can you feel that? His level of devotion seems otherworldly to us. It looks extreme but should be normal. How can anyone realize what has taken place in Christ and walk away unmoved? Paul gave his entire life to defend what he called "the truth of the gospel." This one truth is everything. We have nothing without it. God save us from the peril of forgetting it.

A Grenade Tossed in the Suburb

When Paul wrote the controversy-filled letter of 1 Corinthians, he threw a grenade of awareness into a context not much different from ours. The church at Corinth was the original suburban church. As becomes obvious in the letter, they suffered from the same distractions and pitfalls we do. They were status driven, man fearing, spiritually vague, opportunistic, upwardly mobile, self-serving, socially prejudiced, culturally isolationist, and materially obsessive. First Corinthians is a gospel proclamation to a church battling against the gravitational forces of a sophisticated culture. This is why Paul opens up with the cannon fire of the cross. The church needed to be distracted from its many distractions.

> Christ did not send me to baptize, but to preach the gospel, not in cleverness of speech, that the cross of Christ would not be made void.

> For the word of the cross is foolishness to those who are perishing, but to us who are being saved it is the power of God. For it is written, "I will destroy the wisdom of the wise, and the cleverness of the clever I will set aside." Where is the wise man? Where is the scribe? Where is the debater of this age? Has not God made foolish the wisdom of the world? For since in the wisdom of God the world through its wisdom did not come to know God, God was well-pleased through the foolishness of the message preached to save those who believe. For indeed Jews ask for signs, and Greeks search for wisdom; but we preach Christ crucified, to Jews a stumbling block and to Gentiles foolishness, but to those who are the called, both Jews and Greeks, Christ the power of God and the wisdom of God (1 Corinthians 1:17-24).

A few verses later he becomes even more explicit and reductionistic.

> When I came to you, brethren, I did not come with supe-
> riority of speech or of wisdom, proclaiming to you the tes-
> timony of God. For I determined to know nothing among
> you except Jesus Christ, and Him crucified (1 Corinthians
> 2:1-2).

Why nothing except Christ and Him crucified? Why was Paul's focus so restricted? Why this singular focus on the cross? The reason is that the cross is the only thing that could save them from the bondage of lesser things. When all else fails to get our attention and we wander away from the glory of our redemption, the cross of Christ tracks us down in our idolatry and drags us back to awestruck devastation. It will not let us—even the most upright among us—get away from the fact that we were rescued from a den of wickedness by a holy God. The message of the cross is cannon fire to the redeemed heart, warning us that neglect of the gospel and nominalism is just beyond us and ready to invade.

The reality of the substitutionary death of Christ contained in the cross is like a chain tied around the heart of the believer, anchoring it to grace. But this chain liberates us from our bondage to things that are merely better or moral. The cross is the scratched record of redemption constantly playing in the ear of the church. It is the singular antidote for the contagion of assuming that the gospel has been received. It is everything. And without it there is nothing. When you can't quite put your finger on what's missing, it is always the cross.

I realize I'm vulnerable to criticism of being imbalanced about this. Much is being made right now of the danger of overemphasizing the atonement or reducing the gospel to a matter of individual redemption. Such reductionism ignores the broader events taking place in the redemptive plan of God. As has been pointed out elsewhere, there is more to the gospel than sheer forensic realities. The gospel also includes the recovery of creation and the restoration of God's intended order. There is more being redeemed than the individual. It is bigger than us. The world will be put back as it was. This too results from the work of Christ on the cross.

Accordingly, when we reduce the gospel down to a set of facts to be believed, we are in danger of creating an entirely individual view of redemption or a merely theoretical Christianity. Many suggest that the propensity to focus too tightly on the reality of substitutionary atonement has kept the church from fulfilling its broader ethical and humanitarian obligations throughout the world. I get where these voices are coming from. I agree that the American church has largely neglected its responsibility for compassion. I'm grateful for the recent resurgence in a humanitarian emphasis coming from younger generations in the church.

But honestly, does anyone really think popular Christianity in American is in danger of overemphasizing the substitutionary atonement of Christ? I think not. I contend that the real danger is that popular Christianity is currently losing touch with it. I'm not intending to encourage the myopic tendencies of the traditional church. Rather, I'm arguing against them from the other side. Suburban Christianity has no real apprehension of the details of redemption. Atonement means very little in the day-to-day life of professing evangelicals. Yes, the gospel speaks to more than the atonement of Christ, but it can never be less than this central truth. In the end, the cross remains the core of the Christian message.

I would argue that the self-absorbed spirituality characterizing much of the American church is not the result of focusing too closely on the atonement. That's impossible. Rather, I would suggest that the self-focus in the church limiting our compassion partly results from our disconnection with the true gospel. The more we take the gospel for granted, the less missional we become.

As it is, this disregard for the gospel is epidemic within popular Christianity. We're constantly misplacing and redefining it. We don't even realize we're doing it anymore. It's a way of life. Joe has to walk right up to you and point it out. It's the air we breathe in suburbianity. I hate to be the one to break it to you, but there's nothing particularly Christian about many of our favorite messages and trends circulating in the modern church. So many of the evangelical movements we flock to have nothing at all to do with the real Christ. They have to do with us. The real implications of the gospel are nearly impossible to find anymore, especially at church.

Don't believe me? How many sermons have you heard preached from the Bible laying out patterns for better living? Countless. We assume this is the point of our faith. Better self. Better marriages. Better sex. Better parenting. Better men. Better women. Better children. Better money. Better attitudes. Better communication. Better decisions. Better everything. Steps to do. Principles to employ. Slick packaging. Motivational videos. They're all positive and constructive. But they're also absent any essential connection to the life, death, burial, and resurrection of Jesus Christ. Without this connection, they are just another form of bondage. Is a comfortable life in the suburbs really what Christ has called us to? Is morality our highest calling? Or have we read these things into the story? It's hard to tell anymore. Without the gospel constantly made obvious, these types of messages make the real message a mere footnote.

Much of what we're imbibing is a uniquely Western take on Christ. It has no relevance to the majority of the world's population. You think orphans in Sierra Leone are concerned about our suburban preoccupation with finding one's meaning in life? No. They're wondering where their next meal will come from. Or if God knows they are there at all. The hope contained in the gospel is the only answer that makes sense in their particular plight. To them it's obvious. In the West its absence is conspicuous.

Think back to last Sunday. You probably went to church looking to be inspired and motivated. The sermons you took in most likely offered all kinds of helpful domestic information and tips for living. All of this is well and good. But was there any "Christ and Him crucified"? Did you learn more about what God has done? Did the gospel of Jesus Christ show up at all? Or was it assumed? If it was mentioned, can you pinpoint what it was saving you from? Think back. Did it save you from the consequences of a fallen planet and your own corruption? Or did it sound more like it was designed to save you from being ensnared in an unfulfilled life?

Look, I get it. We're Americans. It's in our blood. We're drawn to practical and immediately applicable types of spiritual-sounding information. We live busy lives. As a result, some finely tuned and helpful messages are being delivered by very gifted communicators sitting unimposingly on stools bathed in soft spotlights. They move us, impress us, and touch us deeply. It's "where the rubber meets the road" kind of information. You walk away encouraged about the potential of your life and the rest of your week.

But did you leave excited about what Christ has done? Did you see your need for Him? Did you walk away a brokenhearted worshipper, grateful for the forgiveness you have in Christ? Were you a leper on your knees, thanking God for His mercy? Or were you a consumer with your hand out? Did you walk away with a hope that will sustain you when your perfectly manicured life falls apart? Were you astonished that Christ offered His life for yours? Did you walk away humbled and motivated by what Christ has accomplished? Did someone point you inward toward your own perceived needs or outward toward God and His incomprehensible grace?

Free Group Therapy and Suburban Christianity

Somewhere along the way we've allowed people in the pew to believe that the gospel was not so much news of a rescue mission executed by God's grace as much as it is a perpetual life-improvement course. To be clear, I believe in sanctification and the progress of change wrought by the Holy Spirit. I believe we are being conformed into the image of Christ. I consider the inner spiritual life of the believer to be critically important. What I cannot believe is that the vague spiritual messages we hear coming from the church are connected to actual biblical realities. They are not the same. It's at this point that we've read American ideals into the Bible. It's a designer redemption.

The church sounds far more like free group therapy than a blessedly redundant celebration of God's redemption of unworthy sinners. The full gospel and all its implications are missing. Its absence has left a strange-sounding silence reverberating in the suburban church. The implicit promise underlying nearly everything we have to offer (sermons, books, video, curriculum, conferences) is clear—your personal happiness and comfort is God's greatest concern. The messages of inner peace, personal fulfillment, and sustained morality have overtaken the language of divine redemption.

The affluence of the American suburbs has hijacked the cross and driven it right into irrelevance. The gospel has been retrofitted to include an unending list of suburban aspirations and preferences. Christ's life, death, and resurrection have all but fallen out of the rotation. The idea of substitution has all but vanished from our vocabulary. There is a hole in our message the size and shape of a dying man. As it is, gospel-less sermons, churches, and ministries abound within suburbianity. There is scant mention of a righteous substitute anymore. This is especially true where I live and pastor.

Fundamentally, Christians will always be sinners saved by grace from the wrath of God through the offering of a righteous substitute. If we are anything, we are the redeemed. We cannot lose sight of this identity. The reality of substitution (Christ put to death as a sacrifice for our sins) distinguishes Christianity from every other message. To remove it from our songs, books, and sermons (by assuming everyone knows about it and has experienced it) is the equivalent of removing a heart from a perfectly healthy person.

Without the implications of the cross—Christ died for sinners—everything we believe completely unravels and ceases to be. There is no Christianity without it. What's left is lifeless and merely practical. To intentionally leave it out of our message is to abandon our message altogether. If you discard the cross of Christ, Christianity is no better than New Age spirituality, hard-core Islamic asceticism, Mormon moralism, or good ol' boy churchianity. There is no Christianity without "Christ and Him crucified."

The late Francis Schaeffer, a Christian apologist and philosopher, shared an illustration of the importance of substitution in the gospel and the message of the church. He imagined sitting beside an unbeliever on a plane that was plummeting to earth. As he imagined it, he had only 60 seconds before impact. In that amount of time he said he would spend 55 seconds describing the problem of man's sin and five seconds describing the solution found in Christ's righteous sacrifice. The one reality (sin) would make the other reality (Christ's death) obvious. Brilliant.

My guess is that if you put a contemporary Christian in that seat next to the unbeliever, the result would be tragic. Five seconds before the plane hit the ground the unbeliever would have no clue how a clearly defined purpose in life would save him from the oncoming planet. What difference does the potential for personal happiness make when you're barreling toward destruction? The cross is the only suitable reality in that moment. What that guy needs to know is that someone offered to sit in his seat for him. Jesus substituted Himself. The rest is peripheral.

Simply ask yourself this question. Did Jesus really need to die in order for human beings to enjoy some level of happiness on earth? Of course not. Therefore, happiness cannot be the fundamental aim of Christianity. The cross insists that He died for much greater realities. The two concepts share no essential relationship.

Jesus did not die for happy marriages because He did not have to die in order for people to have them. Non-Christians experience happy marriages all the time. Contrary to what we might assume, there are plenty of happily married atheists out there. My unsaved Hindu neighbor is one of the more decent men with one of the happiest marriages and some of the most well-behaved kids I've ever met. If this level of happiness is the aim of Christianity, my neighbor has no need for Jesus. In fact, if a life of contentment and comfort is the ultimate goal, the crucifixion of the Son of God was a gross overreaction. As Paul put it, it was in vain.

> I have been crucified with Christ; it is no longer I who live,

> but Christ lives in me; and the life which I now live in the
> flesh I live by faith in the Son of God, who loved me and
> gave Himself for me. I do not set aside the grace of God; for
> if righteousness comes through the Law, then Christ died
> in vain (Galatians 2:20-21).

This is why the cross is indispensable to our message. Substitutionary atonement (the cross) is like a toe tag on a corpse that constantly pokes out from under the sheet of nominalism the popular church has thrown over Christianity. It's always there disturbing our delusion. All our sophistication won't quite reach to cover it.

> Much more then, having now been justified by His blood,
> we shall be saved from the wrath of God through Him.
> For if while we were enemies we were reconciled to God
> through the death of His Son, much more, having been
> reconciled, we shall be saved by His life (Romans 5:9-10).

So, to put it directly, if Christianity is all about cleaner living, personal happiness, inner peace, staying affluent in the suburbs, keeping our kids from bad influences, or finding deeper fulfillment, Jesus is not even necessary. That's not good news. It's merely better. If that's all Christianity is and the reason we get up on Sunday mornings, then I can see exactly why we assume everybody knows this "gospel" and then forgets it. We don't need Jesus to experience any of this. No wonder our messages bear a striking resemblance to motivational speeches and not calls to desperate faith.

These days, the two messages—personal happiness and divine redemption—are virtually indistinguishable from one another. We've nearly completely morphed them. What's resulted is our popular brand of Christianity, which contains nothing uniquely Christian. You could hear the same type of message at a New Age seminar. Think that's too extreme? Here's a sample of messages and themes prevalent in popular Christianity. I've selected topics that drive many of our bestselling books. See if you can find the cross. See if you can tell any difference between these messages and pagan spirituality. Consider this a pop quiz.

Hunger of the Soul

One thing we know for certain: The secret hunger that gnaws at people's souls has nothing to do with externals like money, status, and security. It's the inner person who craves meaning in life, the end of suffering, and answers to the riddles of love, death, God, the soul, good and evil. A life spent on the surface will never answer these questions or satisfy the needs that drive us to ask them.

Love of Others

On the path of devotion, if you can experience even a glimmer of love, it's possible to experience a little more love. When you experience that little more, then the next degree of intensity is possible. Thus, love engenders love until you reach the point of saturation, when you totally merge into divine love.

Personal Focus

You are where your attention takes you. In fact, you are your attention. If your attention is fragmented, you are fragmented. When your attention is in the past, you are in the past. When your attention is in the present moment, you are in the presence of God and God is present in you... Simply be aware of the present, of what you are doing. The presence of God is everywhere, and you have only to consciously embrace it with your attention.

Life Purpose

Everyone has a purpose in life...a unique gift or special talent to give to others. And when we blend this unique talent with service to others, we experience the ecstasy and exultation of our own spirit.

Stewardship and Generosity

It is the intention behind your giving and receiving that is the important thing. The intention should always be to create happiness for the giver and receiver, because happiness is life-supporting and life-sustaining and therefore generates increase. The return is directly proportional to the giving when it is unconditional and from the heart. That is why the act of giving has to be joyful—the frame of mind has to be one in which you feel joy in the very act of giving. Then the energy behind the giving increases many times over.

True Happiness

Most people say, "I'm happy because...I have family and friends, because I have a great job, because I have money and security." All of these reasons for happiness are tenuous; they come and go like a passing breeze. And when happiness eludes us, we seek pleasure through addictive behaviors out of the unconscious hope that we will find joy. External causes of happiness never create real joy.

True Freedom

You break free when you no longer defend your point of view, when you no longer use stereotypes, harbor extreme likes or dislikes toward people you hardly know. You break free when you refuse to follow the impulses of anger and fear, when you act from humility rather than belligerence, when you tread gently rather than with a swagger, when your speech is nurturing rather than scathing, when you choose to express only your love. And how do you know when you are free? You know you are free when you feel happy and at ease instead of fearful and anxious. You know you are free when you are independent of the good and bad opinions of others, when you have relinquished the need to seek approval, when you believe that you are good enough as you are.

Love for God

> In the Old Testament, when the poet of the Song of Solomon rhapsodizes about his love for God, his words gush as romantically as if he were swooning over a woman: You split me, tore my heart open, filled me with love, you poured your spirit into me; I knew you as I know myself. The parallel between a lover's intoxication and a saint's is impossible to miss…"I am in love with loving," St. Augustine declares, echoing the passions of a million secular lovers.

You might be asking yourself, "What's the problem with these messages? They are, after all, very encouraging and generally biblical." Agreed. But what makes them uniquely Christian? How do we know they are Christian at all? We can't really tell. As far as we know they could have come from the pen of the most popular New Age guru in modern times, Deepak Chopra. As a matter of fact, they did. He wrote them all.[1] How tragic. It's almost impossible to distinguish anymore. Unfortunately, there's not much difference between what we're preaching and the messages coming from the world's foremost New Age spiritualist.

Okay, that was a dirty trick. But you get the point. Do you see it now? Believe it or not, Chopra fits very comfortably on our Christian bestseller lists. He would find little objectionable with our sermons and books. As long as we stay away from the implications of the death of Christ, he's all in. All we have to do is minimize the implication of substitution. Without the explicit presence of the gospel, it might as well be New Age mysticism. Even more frightening, popular Christianity has inadvertently ripped off Chopra's favorite teachings. Just to be clear, this is not a compliment.

Breaking Out the Back Door

We have accepted the division between the public sphere of facts and the private sphere of values, an outer realm of nature and history and an inner realm of freedom and spirit. However, where religion and spirituality are typically means of driving us deeper into ourselves, following our "little voice within" or our "inner light," the gospel summons us to look outside of ourselves for the truth about our condition and identity and especially for any hope of redemption. It just does not finally matter what we think, feel, do, or want to be true. We need someone to give us the report. Yet this is just what we do not want: an authoritative source—even God—standing outside of us and above us, telling us how things actually are.

MICHAEL HORTON

Remember the moment it occurred to you that Disney World wasn't a real kingdom full of talking animals? When as a child you caught a glimpse of an employee's entrance and it struck you as strange? "Mickey comes to work? I thought he lived here!" And that's all it took. You began to realize that none of what you had celebrated as a kid was real. From then on you could never quite enjoy it as you had before. You could not help but notice all the wires and cables. One disturbing fact after another broke into your consciousness. A strange awakening was taking place. It became more than obvious that all the kids in It's a Small World were the same androgynous animatron. Fantasy over.

It takes a similar encounter to notice that we're living in some sort of bizarre subculture of Christianity. Much of what we've assumed to be Christian has no essential relationship to Christianity. It's an American (or Western) revision. Wires and cables are everywhere. Popular Christianity is more like a theme park complete with gift shops than a gathering of the redeemed. Coming to see this is very much like stumbling on a break room at the Magic Kingdom and seeing Mickey's head on a table and the man inside the costume eating a sandwich.

What the church is (and always will be) desperate for is hiding right there in the wide open—the gospel of Jesus Christ. We cannot lose sight of its central implication. Regardless of how decent we look, how well we clean up, or where our kids go to school, we are never more than lepers on our knees begging for God's merciful touch of forgiveness. And God is merciful, even to those who think they are beyond the need for mercy.

Our privileged circumstances here in the churches of the American suburbs have shielded us from the dark side of the gospel. "All have sinned and fall short of the glory of God" (Romans 3:23). We seem to forget that "all" includes those without any criminal record (as well as those criminals with means enough to escape).

Stop and look around for a moment. Push pause on your experience of the Christian life and church. I want you to notice something. There's a strange disconnect between what we're saying and what the Bible is saying. Our experience does not square with the Bible's. You'll see it if you look close enough. They're not even remotely similar. Our terms are biblical, but our content is completely different. We're using the Bible's verbiage but telling a much different story.

The Bible is a breathtaking chronicle of God's salvation of sinners. Its pages are filled with a seemingly unending celebration of God's grace, spanning from Genesis to Revelation. It never really moves past this central message. It's not about us. It's primarily about what God has done and is doing. It's about the glorious redemption taking place on this planet. It's unashamedly redundant.

One biblical character after another is driven to worship at the stunning spectacle of God's grace. Consider the book of Acts. The early church is wholly different from what we are. The gospel of Jesus Christ did not merely enhance their lives. It turned them upside down. Paradigms shifted. Worldviews collapsed. Value systems were disemboweled. Less is more. Strength is weakness. Great is small. All are unworthy. All may be saved. No longer was there class, race, or status. A worldwide neighborhood of sinners. There was only Christ.

> With many other words he solemnly testified and kept on exhorting them, saying, "Be saved from this perverse generation!" So then, those who had received his word were baptized; and there were added that day about three thousand souls. And they were continually devoting themselves to the apostles' teaching and to fellowship, to the breaking of bread and to prayer.
>
> Everyone kept feeling a sense of awe; and many wonders and signs were taking place through the apostles. And all those who had believed were together and had all things in common; and they began selling their property and possessions and were sharing them with all, as anyone might have need. And day by day continuing with one mind in the temple, and breaking bread from house to house, they were taking their meals together with gladness and sincerity of heart, praising God, and having favor with all the people. And the Lord was adding to their number day by day those who were being saved (Acts 2:40-47).

The reality of the risen Lord fell like a bomb on ancient Jerusalem and sent shock waves across the world. One morning unsuspecting individuals went to work, and that afternoon they returned home completely different people. They looked the same but weren't. A riot erupted in their souls. They were overthrowing the status quo. This power spread from one heart to another. The church exploded onto the planet.

Our Christianity is patently different. If you compare the two, the difference is undeniable. We're not really looking for the gospel to dismantle our lives. Instead, we're looking for it to improve them. Our churches no longer explode upon cultures; they assimilate into them. Unlike the biblical characters who can't quite get over the history of redemption, we obsess about the potential of our temporal existence. In our world, Christ is more like an addendum on an otherwise good life and not a life-altering encounter. Jesus is more the logical choice here in the suburbs. Believing in Jesus is what civilized, well-educated people do to round off their existence.

Christianity in the burbs is primarily about how each of us can be delivered from a vague existence, directionless life, unreached potential, or unclear purpose on earth. This is where the disconnect is the greatest. We've been conditioned to think Christianity is about locating God's specific will for our lives. This thread is everywhere in our story. Out there somewhere is an amazing life God has for you. Jesus came to help us find it. The clichés supporting this emphasis dominate our evangelical airwaves. "Your life can have an impact." "You can make a new start." "You can be victorious." "God saved you for significance." All of this is almost entirely detached from the biblical reality.

Once your eyes are opened to the scandal of the Son of God on the cross, you immediately realize the majority of the stuff we're assuming as evangelicals has nothing to do with true Christianity. It simply cannot square.

Suburbianity was created to distract us from what's real. We're all unsuspectingly trapped in an evangelical version of *The Truman Show*. You have to make a break for it and bust out the back of this odd production to find freedom. Once outside, the slightest glimpse of the biblical reality makes the fantasy obvious. The cross of Christ busts you out. Once you see the cross for what it truly is, you can never quite enjoy the fantasy. The cross of Christ is a boot on the front door of suburbianity. The cross of Christ is an elephant in the church.

Think about it. The cross—the fundamental symbol of Christianity—is a rather brutal condemnation of our feel-good Christianese.

The cross hangs there in our churches and heckles our jargon-filled sermons and ridiculous sound bites. It's a protester lingering outside our services, handing out a truth contrary to what we just heard. It calls every one of us out—despite all our niceties and decorum. We are all vicious people deserving the harshest punishment the universe has to offer. If the death of Christ has real atoning value, you cannot escape this conclusion. After all, He atoned for you. Face it. We're so evil, only the crucifixion of the incarnate Son of God could atone for our sins.

No one can truly behold the cross and maintain the illusions the popular church promotes. According to Calvary, our greatest need is not a better marriage, an improved self-image, financial success, or any other of the suburban daydreams. It's reconciliation to a holy God. Jesus is not our buddy, personal Oprah, or spiritual self-help coach. Jesus is sent on a radical rescue mission by a radically gracious God. Rescue from what? Not your melancholy state of mind, but from the consequence of you. We deserve eternal damnation (a thought slightly beyond melancholy). That is the straight-up, brutally honest message of the ever-present intervention of the cross. That symbol we wear so haphazardly as jewelry is more a declaration of guilt than a token of devotion. Your rescue from ruin required the death of the Son of God. There is no good in you. That's what the cross is saying.

> "There is none righteous, not even one;
> There is none who understands,
> There is none who seeks for God;
> All have turned aside, together they have become useless;
> There is none who does good,
> There is not even one."
> "Their throat is an open grave,
> With their tongues they keep deceiving,"
> "The poison of asps is under their lips;"
> "Whose mouth is full of cursing and bitterness;"
> "Their feet are swift to shed blood,
> Destruction and misery are in their paths,

And the path of peace have they not known."
"There is no fear of God before their eyes" (Romans
3:10-18).

The Unrelenting Pressure of Keeping Up Appearances

The suburbs produce a Stepford Christianity. It's plastic. We meander back and forth between our routines, keeping up the appearance of perfection. The pressure that the suburbs place on human beings in general and on Christians in particular is hard to measure. Many in my own congregation have caved under the weight. Our marriages are expected to be storybook. Our kids are expected to be poster children. Our stuff is expected to be new. Keeping up appearances is a full-time job. It can also be suffocating. You get the sense that the average Christian in the pew is ready to stand up and scream, "I'm not perfect! My marriage struggles! My teenager is using drugs! My husband's job is in jeopardy! I'm coming apart at the seams and trying to keep up! Can someone help me? Please!"

The truth of the cross is our breakout moment. Outside, reality sets in. Our marriages aren't perfect and never will be regardless of how many weekend marriage conferences we attend. Not this side of glory. Our spouse is not the problem with our marriage. Sin is. Our kids will never obey us the way we want them to—regardless of the number of books on parenting we read. God does not want us to be rich. He may want us to be poor.

Non-Christians aren't the enemy. They're the point. We cannot achieve perpetual and unending happiness on this earth through possessions, a sense of purpose, or uninterrupted contentment. Suffering is real. Furthermore, suffering is not a sign of God's disfavor. It's simply a sign of reality. After all, this is a fallen planet. Unplugged from popular Christianity, these become obvious facts. That family in the frame is a myth. In ways too numerous to count, our brand of Christianity is actually a denial of biblical Christianity.

Joe pointed me to the door, and grace kicked the door off its hinges. When it did, the transformation of my perspective was almost immediate. The weight began to lift. Unending treasures of grace that I had taken for granted for so long flooded into my life and soul. I had been aware of grace the entire time, but it lay around like clutter on the floor of my Christianity. The experience was like falling in love with my wife again. I had loved her all along but had forgotten to tell her or to enjoy the romance. Jesus became new.

Turning Reality Right Side Up

To be clear, I'm no ogre. I realize I sound cynical. I'm not. I'm overjoyed. I know what a fresh grasp of the gospel can do for the church. Fact is, I want people to be happy and better and moral and decent and fulfilled and successful. My aim is not to deny Christians any of these aspects of faith and practice. I realize I may come off sounding like a spiritual hall monitor, but I'm not. I don't intend to deny the additional realities that accompany the effect of the gospel—love for your neighbor, personal transformation, compassion for the needy. Indeed, these are the ripple effects of the gospel's power dropped in a shoreless reality of grace.

Christianity is not drudgery. It's joyous freedom. I'm pretty certain I can defend this biblically. I don't want to rob people of the positive spiritual experiences resulting from the practice of their faith. I'm not aiming at prudish irrelevance. In fact, what I hope to demonstrate is exactly the opposite. Real relevance. The message of the Bible applies to every person on the planet. That's relevant. It transcends levels of incomes and status in society. The problem with the guy behind the picket fence and the guy in the gutter is the same. According to the Bible, we're all saved out of the gutter and destined for streets of gold. To get where we need to be, every last one of us must view himself more like a leper and less middle-class.

A true and untouchable joy that surpasses all previous experience is possible if we will but take our eyes off ourselves for a moment and place them on the glories of Christ. We desperately need to reverse the thinking of popular Christianity by making it less about the Christian and more about Christ. We need to move our language from first person (I, me, mine) to third person (He, His, Him). We need to de-clutter the cross and get our eyes on it. Ultimately, the bliss everyone seems to be looking for can come only from the awareness of grace. It's a by-product of a much greater reality.

I don't want to deceive people by preaching a message that has them assuming their lives will improve if they turn to Christ. Christ did not die to accomplish this in the popular manner of speaking. Ultimately, it may get worse. Jesus may ask you for everything you love.

> If anyone wishes to come after Me, he must deny himself, and take up his cross and follow Me. For whoever wishes to save his life will lose it, but whoever loses his life for My sake and the gospel's will save it. For what does it profit a man to gain the whole world, and forfeit his soul? For what will a man give in exchange for his soul? For whoever is ashamed of Me and My words in this adulterous and sinful generation, the Son of Man will also be ashamed of him when He comes in the glory of His Father with the holy angels (Mark 8:34-38).

I want us to understand that the aim of Christ's death—the satisfaction of the righteous demands of God and the propitiation of our sins—actually results in a joy and peace that boggles the mind. The awareness of Christ's willing sacrifice of His life for mine produces impenetrable peace.

> Blessed be the God and Father of our Lord Jesus Christ, who according to His great mercy has caused us to be born again to a living hope through the resurrection of Jesus Christ from the dead, to obtain an inheritance which is imperishable and undefiled and will not fade away, reserved in heaven for you, who are protected by the power of God through faith for a salvation ready to be revealed in the last time. In this you greatly rejoice, even though now for a little while, if necessary, you have been distressed by various trials, that the proof of your faith, being more precious

than gold which is perishable, even though tested by fire, may be found to result in praise and glory and honor at the revelation of Jesus Christ; and though you have not seen Him, you love Him, and though you do not see Him now, but believe in Him, you greatly rejoice with joy inexpressible and full of glory, obtaining as the outcome of your faith the salvation of your souls (1 Peter 1:3-9).

Inexpressible joy can be had by no other means than a growing awareness and deeper application of the story of redemption. Happiness in light of the cross is very different from happiness in light of happiness. One is untouchable. The other is momentary, rust-covered, and moth-eaten. Our treasures are in heaven, not here. Jesus made this clear.

Do not store up for yourselves treasures on earth, where moth and rust destroy, and where thieves break in and steal. But lay up for yourselves treasures in heaven, where neither moth nor rust destroys, and where thieves do not break in or steal; for where your treasure is, there will your heart be also (Matthew 6:19-21).

Our evangelical narcissism is robbing us of the very joy we desire. We're missing the liberation of soul found in a fresh discovery of God's grace. All we long for is there in the gospel. This is especially true for consumer-driven Christians. Somehow we fail to understand this.

If asked to explain the particulars of God's act of redemption in Christ, its contours and layers, most Christians struggle for words. We know far more about what we're doing than what God has done. But Christianity is not primarily inwardly focused. It is primarily outwardly focused. It is focused on a righteousness that lies outside of who we are and not on a potential for improved lives. Our real delight is found outside of us.

I count all things to be loss in view of the surpassing value of knowing Christ Jesus my Lord, for whom I have suffered

the loss of all things, and count them but rubbish so that
I may gain Christ, and may be found in Him, not having
a righteousness of my own derived from the Law, but that
which is through faith in Christ, the righteousness which
comes from God on the basis of faith, that I may know
Him and the power of His resurrection and the fellowship
of His sufferings, being conformed to His death; in order
that I may attain to the resurrection from the dead (Philippians 3:8-11).

Nothing is more counterintuitive to suburban Christians than
the gospel of Jesus Christ. Jesus Christ and Him crucified has a way
of turning everything on its ear. Up is down. Happiness is suffering.
Wealth is poverty. Power is servitude. Contentment is abandonment.
When viewed in light of the gospel, the truth is usually the opposite
of whatever we're thinking at the time here in the suburbs.

- Our problem is not a want of purpose, or sadness resulting from less than preferred earthly circumstances. This
  is the gospel of the suburbs. Our problem is a sinful and
  idolatrous heart, which seeks its happiness in everything
  except its Creator. This is the truth flowing out of the
  gospel.

- Happy marriages don't result from one spouse making
  the other spouse happier. This is the gospel of the suburbs. Happy marriages result when both spouses die to
  self and view themselves as unworthy of one another.
  This is the truth flowing out of the gospel.

- Deepest satisfaction in life does not come with the perfect house and enough disposable income to do what we
  want. This is the gospel of the suburbs. Deepest satisfaction comes when we abandon any hope that the perfect
  house and disposable income will satisfy us. This is the
  truth flowing out of the gospel.

- Life is not about me. This is the gospel of the suburbs. It
  is about the Lord Jesus Christ. This is the true gospel.

The cross turns reality right side up. We don't need to marginalize the cross—we need to stare into it. It's just so hard to find anymore.

Gospel Flash Mobs

Right now a gospel flash mob is underway in evangelicalism. All at once, people are unassuming the gospel. Making the gospel obvious and applicable is now revolutionary. Without warning, people have begun to gather around any preacher or author who refuses to assume that people know the gospel of Jesus Christ. The most decent-looking people are acting like lepers.

People have been let out the back door of suburbianity and into the warm light of reality. Multiple generations of Christians are rediscovering the power of the cross and gazing on the unmatched beauty of Christ's righteous sacrifice. All things are new. It's as if making the gospel central is a novel idea.

Gospel-focused churches (an ironic way to describe them) are filling up with Christians young and old. Most are not looking for the latest craze; they are desperate for a formerly assumed message made clear. It is very different from the herds that chased every church-in-a-box trend that came along. The messages people are flocking to aren't Christian-lite messages about becoming people of influence or motivational speeches about life purpose. They're relentless gospel bombs being tossed at the Christian's propensity for assuming the best about self and losing sight of the real purpose of Christ's death. It's not less accountability, but more. It's not ease, but self-sacrifice. It's not superficial remedies, but repentance and surrender on an unequaled level. They are cross-saturated and grace-filled declarations of God's triumph in Christ. They aren't looking for the latest craze, but the same old story.

After spending decades caught between the powerless options of self-help spirituality and shortsighted moralism, Christians are having their souls filled with a new awareness of God's grace in Christ. Moralism and pragmatism—stemming from the same root of self-justification—are now unmasked as the mortal enemies of the grace of God.

No longer are Christians taking the gospel for granted. They're reveling in its redundancy. The righteous work of God accomplished outside of us in Christ has the undivided attention of those souls left thirsty by bestsellers and self-help principles. Innumerable broken-hearted worshippers are finding their only joy and consolation in the unending celebration of the one thing God has done in Christ. For them, the gospel is not something you get past. It is something in which you get lost. "God is love" is no longer a slogan of weak-stomached Christianity, but a mind-blowing demonstration of the power of God to save sinners. Everyone seems to be bumping into each other coming around corners on the road to Emmaus.

No wonder. The world is not what it once was. The naïveté of previous Christian generations has been interrupted by nonstop updates of reality flowing from the information age. Images from all over the world have washed up on our perfectly manicured shores here in the West. We can no longer hide safely behind Christian walls the way we once did. It is a sinful and broken world out there. The fantasy is blown. Neither moralism nor pragmatism has helped protect us.

Sex trafficking is no longer reserved for far-off lands, but is next door. Genocide is headline news. Energy crises abound. Political corruption is expected. Sex scandals are the norm. Pornography is epidemic. Half of all marriages collapse. Children worlds away die of starvation while we toss excess into the trash. AIDS ravages entire continents. Young men and women scarred by combat in an endless war are returning home devastated. Kids relentlessly bullied at school commit suicide out of despair. Teenage girls pressured by the myth of perfection injure themselves out of anger. "Normal" people walk onto college campuses and shoot dozens of innocent people. Economies rupture and take fortunes down with them. Cancer shows up unexpectedly in the healthiest of people. Fathers and mothers walk away from families. Planes fly into iconic buildings. Monuments to prosperity crumble and become memorials to hate.

These realities have always existed. But the church in the suburbs was determined to shield itself from them. We chose to focus on more acceptable problems in the safety of our conclaves. Slight problems requiring only delicate remedies. This delusion is no longer. The cross is not for the faint of heart. Reality climbed over our walls and kicked in our doors. Furthermore, we now realize that isolating ourselves from the rest of the world only served to lock us in with the real enemy—our wicked hearts. The answer to the problem underlying all these issues has been here the entire time—the gospel of God, the act of redemption. Some people who were long existing in the hazy spirituality of popular Christianity are beginning to get it.

Those who do get it do so partly because the superficial answers provided by evangelicalism have failed them. People are rushing out of traditional churches, bludgeoned by moralism on one side and pragmatism on the other. The principles and lists they've been handed over the years in church resulted in a strange sort of bondage to the fascination of self-improvement. Regardless of how hard they've tried, they can't quite get there. The practical steps are no match for the truth lying beneath the surface. They are keenly aware that their personal issues are deeper than the average sermon or book suggests. We are "deceitfully wicked." We are broken and sinful people. Imperfect people who look nothing like the people they have been told they should resemble. Marriages struggle. Kids rebel. Addictions creep in. No wonder people are flocking to good news. Better news is useless.

What's most striking about the migration within evangelicalism is the number of people walking away from biblical churches to join other biblical churches making concerted efforts to focus on the fundamental themes of redemption. Reasonable, mature, and well-adjusted Christians in their middle years are leaving churches of their youth. Why? They've seen the wires and cables. They've noticed the hole in the message. They cannot un-notice it. They are ruined. So much has been assumed. Those who grew up in conservative churches feel as if they've been shortchanged by the neglect of the message of grace. The model of ministry they've been given assumes that those outside the confines of church are the ones who need the gospel. They now know better.

Not long after seeing it for myself, I stood up and apologized to my people for laying a burden on them not even their forefathers could bear. I literally repented publicly for overlooking the gospel. I had been pointing my dearest friends to themselves and not to Christ. All at once, I became an evangelist to those both inside and outside of the church. It was a burden. As the saying goes, there are two ways to unload a gun. I chose the one involving the trigger. My heart went off in the church. At first they did not understand all I meant, but they did know how deeply I meant it. I exhorted them through tears. Before long, they would come to understand. The effect was transformative, disruptive, and everything in between.

A young stay-at-home mom who grew up as the daughter of a fundamentalist pastor sat stunned week after week. "But I've always thought…" A Christian couple in their sixties who'd been in church all their lives and graduated from a conservative Bible college wept with me at dinner. "How have we missed this?" A man in his seventies who'd served faithfully in church for decades encouraged me. "I don't know what you are doing, but keep doing it." A dad with a well-informed and robust reformed theology realized he had no real affection for the person of Christ. "I've gone from hearing to seeing." A former stripper who once was ashamed of her past was liberated by the unrelenting message of righteousness in Christ. "I cannot believe I'm forgiven." A homeschool kid misled by the virtue of his upbringing repented like a former stripper. "I cannot believe I am forgiven." A man having committed multiple affairs over 40 years of marriage repented so deeply and totally that his wife was swept off her feet with forgiveness. "I feel like I've been married for six months." What they all had in common was the discovery of the truth hiding in the wide open of the church—the gospel.

Not all reactions were positive. Many conservative-minded people whom I love and agree with theologically became concerned about the redundant message and change of tone coming from the pulpit.

Many of them left. The deconstruction was too uncomfortable. Others who were more inclined to popular Christianity expressed unease about the belligerently negative assessment of human beings and call to lordship. Many of this mindset also left.

I completely understood why they were leaving. They were not wrong. It was a tumultuous time. Some confronted me, "When are you going to stop focusing on the cross? When are we going to move on to more practical matters?" Others expressed their concern to my elders. "Can we emphasize something besides grace? Can we move on to something else?" I get what they are saying. But I wondered at the time (and still do), "On to what?" I'm never going back.

> "For this reason I have said to you, that no one can come to Me, unless it has been granted him from the Father."
>
> As a result of this many of His disciples withdrew and were not walking with Him anymore. Jesus said to the twelve, "You do not want to go away also, do you?" Simon Peter answered Him, "Lord, to whom shall we go? You have words of eternal life. We have believed and have come to know that You are the Holy One of God" (John 6:65-69).

A Note to My Fellow Exegetes

"You hypocrites, rightly did Isaiah prophesy of you, saying, 'This people honors Me with their lips, but their heart is far away from Me. But in vain do they worship Me, teaching as doctrines the precepts of men.'" After Jesus called the crowd to Him, He said to them, "Hear and understand. It is not what enters into the mouth that defiles the man, but what proceeds out of the mouth, this defiles the man."

MATTHEW 15:7-11

Sermons Every Mormon Could Enjoy

You might think I'm reserving my criticism for the fluffy, pragmatic types who drift away from traditional church models. Honestly, they're easy targets. Certainly, the talking heads of the health, wealth, and prosperity movement are guilty of assuming everyone knows the gospel (and of reinventing it)—pretty much constantly. And those life-coach guys of the seeker movement with frosted tips and cowboy-cut pearl-button shirts—who should be selling squeegees on TV—are among the worst offenders. They drive me crazy. But actually, I'm just as concerned about those who assume they're not assuming the gospel.

Those who are most committed to an unaccommodating gospel have accommodated it by assuming that its message applies to other people or that it isn't relevant for their day-to-day existence. This is not some haphazard sweeping generalization. This is me. It's where I live. It happens all the time. My familiarity with the Bible allows me to assume that the truth and demands of the gospel apply to someone else—the unsaved, liberals, secularists, or Democrats—but not me. I assume that what the cross says about humanity's true condition, it's saying to someone else. Self-righteousness is my personal clutter.

Forgetting what God has done for His people is the keynote in our history. From the very beginning God put the idea of a substitute in our way to remind us of our constant need. The Passover was put in Israel's path to keep them back from the ledge of forgetfulness and its severe consequences.

> "The LORD will pass through to smite the Egyptians; and when He sees the blood on the lintel and on the two door-posts, the LORD will pass over the door and will not allow the destroyer to come in to your houses to smite you. And you shall observe this event as an ordinance for you and your children forever. When you enter the land which the LORD will give you, as He has promised, you shall observe this rite. And when your children say to you, 'What does this rite mean to you?' you shall say, 'It is a Passover sacrifice to the LORD who passed over the houses of the sons of Israel in Egypt when He smote the Egyptians, but spared our homes.'" And the people bowed low and worshiped (Exodus 12:23-27).

Every time his people lost sight of their deliverance, the worship of the one true God morphed into an indistinguishable amalgam of self-help spirituality. What resulted was something left over from Egypt and picked up from every pagan nation they encountered thereafter. Right after the exodus from Egypt, God declared, "See what I have done for you?" His people kindly replied, "Thanks for that. Now, look what we came up with to get us the rest of the way."

> Now when the people saw that Moses delayed to come down from the mountain, the people assembled about Aaron and said to him, "Come, make us a god who will go before us; as for this Moses, the man who brought us up

from the land of Egypt, we do not know what has become of him." Aaron said to them, "Tear off the gold rings which are in the ears of your wives, your sons, and your daughters, and bring them to me." Then all the people tore off the gold rings which were in their ears and brought them to Aaron. He took this from their hand, and fashioned it with a graving tool and made it into a molten calf; and they said, "This is your god, O Israel, who brought you up from the land of Egypt." Now when Aaron saw this, he built an altar before it; and Aaron made a proclamation and said, "Tomorrow shall be a feast to the LORD." So the next day they rose early and offered burnt offerings, and brought peace offerings; and the people sat down to eat and to drink, and rose up to play (Exodus 32:1-6).

That's us. Melting down the glories of God's grace and shaping them into something of our own imagination. We are constantly turning our backs on the incredible reality of the cross for smaller ones that get us nowhere. Like our predecessors, we're always moving on. We have an uncanny knack for overlooking the astonishing miracle of deliverance at our backs and the amazing grace out in front of us.

Our Lord knew we'd do this. Before His death, Jesus established a meal for His followers celebrating His atoning death.

While they were eating, Jesus took some bread, and after a blessing, He broke it and gave it to the disciples, and said, "Take, eat; this is My body." And when He had taken a cup and given thanks, He gave it to them, saying, "Drink from it, all of you; for this is My blood of the covenant, which is poured out for many for forgiveness of sins. But I say to you, I will not drink of this fruit of the vine from now on until that day when I drink it new with you in My Father's kingdom" (Matthew 26:26-29).

Not surprisingly, it's a redeployment of the Passover meal. Jesus co-opted that vision, fulfilled it, and set it as a perpetual memorial for

His followers. Same message—*remember*. Throughout the church's history, Christians have corporately celebrated the Lord's Table, drawing on its implications as often as they observe it. I'm not sure the majority of us understand the point. We do it more because we're supposed to than because we're inclined to.

Some see Communion primarily as a moment for introspection and spiritual centering. For others it's more sentimental, and they view Jesus as more of a helpless victim than a willing sacrifice. Others, filled with guilt at their inability to act like good people, walk out of church determined to do better until next time—as if by "It is finished," Christ actually meant, "It's nearly done." Still others see it as an essential means of salvation mediated through the church. Ultimately, these last two perspectives end in the same place—a denial of the very point behind the image. It actually *is* finished.

But a question remains. Of all things, why order us to remember His death? Why not His birth? Why not His miracles? Why not His teaching? Why not His acts of kindness toward the needy? Why not His lifestyle? Why the offering of His life and His substitutionary death?

He told us to remember His death because it is the only reality that won't allow us to take the gospel of grace for granted. It is the thing without which Christianity ceases to exist. As has already been stated, His substitutionary sacrifice is everything and the one thing that distinguishes Christianity from every attempt at self-salvation out there.

The Lord's Table is an explicit declaration that man cannot save himself and that God saves by radical grace through the sacrifice of His son. How ironic. We are required to do one thing so we will remember that Jesus met the requirements for us.

> After saying above, "Sacrifices and offerings and whole burnt offerings and sacrifices for sin You have not desired, nor have You taken pleasure in them" (which are offered according to the Law), then He said, "Behold, I have come to do Your will." He takes away the first in order to establish

the second. By this will we have been sanctified through the offering of the body of Jesus Christ once for all.

Every priest stands daily ministering and offering time after time the same sacrifices, which can never take away sins; but He, having offered one sacrifice for sins for all time, sat down at the right hand of God, waiting from that time onward until His enemies be made a footstool for His feet. For by one offering He has perfected for all time those who are sanctified (Hebrews 10:8-14).

The Lord's Table was inserted in our worship as a sort of speed bump on our way to taking the gospel for granted. It is a deterrent against forgetting the objective realities contained in the gospel. It is an image of what God has done in reality. A constant reminder of a singular truth—in His Son, God saves wretches. By grace through faith alone. The Lord's Table declutters our worship of Christ. It is a redundant message on a loop built into the system of the redeemed. It's a reminder that what saves us from the consequence of the corruption inside us lies outside us in the righteous sacrifice of the life of Christ. The Lord's Table protects us from the toxic habit of taking the gospel for granted. Or of assuming we had anything to do with it. We can't escape this reality.

I come from a church heritage that's dead serious about the Bible. How serious? We practically take credit for it. In fact, we refer to ourselves historically as the Bible church movement. The church I pastor is a direct descendant of this movement. Every week I have the distinct privilege of taking the Bible at face value. It is an honor to stand in this tradition. Remember those liberals from a hundred years ago from across the pond who infiltrated the seminaries here in the states? Those seminaries were part of historically reformed and conservative denominations. Through them liberalism infiltrated thousands of churches across the country. Eventually, pastors showed up in their pulpits denying everything the denomination had historically confessed. The Bible is not the Word of God. Jesus is not God. There is no such thing as sin. Jesus did not die as an atonement for sin.

Jesus was not raised from the dead. Faithful, God-fearing people fled these denominations seeking the truth. Independent churches rose up, determined to return to the Bible. Hence the Bible church movement. Bible defended. Truth established. That was us. We did it!

But we who respect the Bible the most are the ones I'm most concerned about. Why? Not because we deny the truth, but because a hundred years after battling for it we too are taking it for granted. Conservative evangelicals who will have nothing to do with the pitfalls of pragmatism are in danger of ending in the same place pragmatists have—gospel-less messages. In many ways we are the worst offenders. We love to point out the empty self-help rhetoric of the more popular health and wealth propagators, but we would be horrified to realize that many of our messages match theirs in ineffectiveness—they are powerless to save or change anyone. In their message, Christ is buried under the rhetoric of self-help. In ours, Christ is buried under the rhetoric of the Bible. Fact is, you can listen to very biblical sermons and never catch a glimpse of Christ and Him crucified. In our world Jesus isn't merchandise to sell. He's more like a secret handshake.

It is possible to love, study, teach, preach, and read the Bible and completely miss its point—*Christ*. We've got the facts of the Bible nailed while ignoring the truth behind the nails driven into His hands and feet. It's as if we have an incredible jewel—the person and work of Jesus Christ—but rather than drawing attention to its beauty, we fastidiously obsess over the details of the setting and clasps beneath it. Those details are essential. I thrive on those details. But those details are there because they hold up a much greater truth—the gospel. We seem never to look up and be awestruck at the unmatched glory of the person and work of Christ.

Preaching is nothing more and nothing less than the systematic disclosure of the profound mysteries and details of the gospel revealed in the Bible. Paul described himself as a steward of one message.

> Let a man regard us in this manner, as servants of Christ, and stewards of the mysteries of God. In this case, moreover, it is required of stewards that one be found trustworthy (1 Corinthians 4:1-2).

The Bible as a unit is about the gospel, so preaching from the Bible must center on this main theme. After all, Jesus declared that the Bible was about Him. "If you believed Moses, you would believe Me; for he wrote of Me" (John 5:46).

His disciples also understood Jesus to be the plot of the Scripture. "Philip found Nathanael and said to him, 'We have found Him of whom Moses in the Law and also the Prophets wrote—Jesus of Nazareth, the son of Joseph'" (John 1:45).

When Paul was describing the essence of Abraham's faith and the promise God made to the patriarch, he made a startling revelation. "The Scripture, foreseeing that God would justify the Gentiles by faith, preached the gospel beforehand to Abraham, saying, 'All the nations will be blessed in you'" (Galatians 3:8).

The gospel was back there in the promise made to Abraham. It was in seed form, but it was the very same message that we have today. Where we stand and preach, we have much more detail. As will be discussed later, the entirety of Scripture is the message of the gospel of God in Christ. You cannot get around it. In one way or another, regardless of where we are and what we are reading or preaching, we are engaging that same message and stringing together pieces of the same plotline.

Unfortunately, it's very common to listen to exegetically sound, Bible-based preaching and never hear the fundamental message of the Bible. There are morals, politics, warnings of poor lifestyle choices, torchings of straw men, exegetical details, principles for righteous living, and a lot of preaching about preaching, but no gospel. Our defenses of the truth are just as likely to obscure Christ's sacrifice as are the sound bites of seeker advocates. The only real difference is that one has killer PowerPoint and the other thinks PowerPoint will send you to hell. Ultimately, they both miss the point. "Preach the truth!" we declare to the pragmatist. But "The truth about what?" is the question that comes back to us from the Bible itself. It's all taken for granted.

When you attempt to explain this concern to those who love the Bible and conservative worship, they look at you like you're crazy. Not unlike the way I looked at Joe when he walked away from me. "We're taking the gospel for granted" makes little sense to people who care deeply about the Bible. No doubt they're thinking, "I love the Bible and Christ. The liberals and seeker types are the ones who endanger the gospel." The first impulse is to do a better job of mentioning it at the end of their sermons. They think that's what I mean.

Ultimately, there's no difference between the effect of corrupting the gospel (popular evangelicalism) and taking it for granted (conservative evangelicalism). Each damns people. With one, the listeners are left to assume that Jesus is not sufficient to save. With the other, the listeners are left to assume that *they* are. This latter tendency has always been the problem with God's devotees. We always move past any vital awareness of the gospel and get lost in the details that support it. Forest for trees kind of stuff.

Pragmatists tell people what they can become while neglecting to tell them who they truly are—helpless sinners. We don't do that, but our neglect is even more damaging. We tell people what they shouldn't be doing (morality) and forget to tell them what Christ has accomplished for them. If we're not constantly circling back to the righteousness of Christ, we're only preaching a better brand of moralism. For certain, Deepak Chopra would walk out on us. But we should take little comfort in this. Chances are good Mormons would feel right at home. It all depends on the Sunday. Regardless of how conservative we are, if our sermons would fit well in a Jewish synagogue, we have ceased being Christian.

It's Impossible to Overemphasize Jesus

Those in this group may argue that this is too reductionistic. I suppose it could be taken this way. But the Bible itself is reductionistic. If I were going to be accused of something, I'd be most comfortable being accused of making a big deal about the Bible's continuity in the gospel. Some people will ask, "But is every sermon supposed to be about the gospel?" In a real sense, *yes*. I've no real hesitation in affirming this premise. In fact, I don't see how it can be otherwise. It is all about Christ anyway. I realize there are innumerable biblical facts and questions to deal with. I'm not denying the various contexts of the biblical books, biblical theology, or biblical history. I'm not proposing some vague system of interpretation. When Paul referred to "Christ and Him crucified," he was not denying the various aspects of theology that accompany the cross.

But we fail to realize that in one way or another, every book of the Bible gets us to (and into) the promise fulfilled in Jesus—the gospel. Genesis to Revelation is about what God did and is doing in Christ. At some places the Bible gives us a 30,000-foot view (as in the Old Testament histories), and at other times it plummets to ten inches off the deck (as in the New Testament epistles). But every book of the Bible is a description of events leading up to or disclosing Jesus and the implications of His life, death, and resurrection.

We may encounter historic figures involved in bringing events to pass. We may read testimonies of fulfillment and predictions of His coming from the mouth of prophets centuries before He arrived. But it is all a depiction, explanation, defense, articulation, and application of the gospel. All of it. The Bible is either revealing it, explaining it, defending it, or encouraging us to live in light of it. It all leads to Christ. And not in some generic way that a New Age guru would be comfortable with either. It all leads to His work on the cross on behalf of sinners.

Consider the New Testament. Every single book in the New Testament is ultimately about the gospel—no exceptions. Every one of these books was written as an articulation and explanation of the work of Christ and its effects in the world through the church. The gospel is what we're reading regardless of the specific chapter we're in or the detail on which we're focused. In other words, the context for everything we study in the New Testament is the gospel.

This includes all the ethical sections we love to focus on. Those sections are applications of the righteous life of Christ to the daily existence of believers. When Paul described Christian marriage and the harmony that should characterize it, he pointed to the cross of Christ.

> Wives, be subject to your own husbands, as to the Lord.
> For the husband is the head of the wife, as Christ also is
> the head of the church, He Himself being the Savior of
> the body. But as the church is subject to Christ, so also the
> wives ought to be to their husbands in everything.
>
> Husbands, love your wives, just as Christ also loved the
> church and gave Himself up for her (Ephesians 5:22-25).

When Peter wanted to encourage persecuted Christians to remain faithful in the midst of pain, he too pointed to the gospel.

> You have been called for this purpose, since Christ also suf-
> fered for you, leaving you an example for you to follow in
> His steps, who committed no sin, nor was any deceit found
> in His mouth; and while being reviled, He did not revile
> in return; while suffering, He uttered no threats, but kept
> entrusting Himself to Him who judges righteously; and
> He Himself bore our sins in His body on the cross, so that
> we might die to sin and live to righteousness; for by His
> wounds you were healed (1 Peter 2:21-24).

When the apostle Paul strengthened believers in their battle with indwelling sin, he did not simply say, "Try harder." He exposed them to the glorious reality of the gospel of Jesus.

> Now if we have died with Christ, we believe that we shall
> also live with Him, knowing that Christ, having been
> raised from the dead, is never to die again; death no longer
> is master over Him. For the death that He died, He died to
> sin once for all; but the life that He lives, He lives to God.
> Even so consider yourselves to be dead to sin, but alive to
> God in Christ Jesus.
>
> Therefore do not let sin reign in your mortal body that
> you should obey its lusts, and do not go on presenting the
> members of your body to sin as instruments of unrigh-
> teousness; but present yourselves to God as those alive from

the dead, and your members as instruments of righteousness to God (Romans 6:8-13).

These letters were all written with the gospel leading the way. Failing to mention the greater context of the gospel—salvation by grace through faith in the finished work of Christ—immediately reduces our preaching to loosely connected data and moralism.

Church is not composed of a group of morally superior people who have figured it out and are now going about the business of hanging on until Jesus gets back. Church is about understanding, dissecting, and absorbing the singular truth of the gospel and applying its bottomless mysteries to every part of our life and existence. The gospel is everything. No unbeliever should ever walk through our doors without having heard it preached. More importantly, no *believer* should ever walk through our doors without having heard it applied to him or her. Every sermon should be about the gospel because every jot and tittle in the Bible is about Jesus. The Bible never takes the gospel for granted. The gospel *is* the Bible.

Gospel-less yet biblical messages offer morality. That is the best and the worst they can do. Placing your faith in the potential of moral reform is damning. Morals point you to you. But you cannot save yourself. Achieving a certain level of morality can only make you feel as if you have no need to be saved—and as if everyone else does. Sermons extolling the virtues of morality are the equivalent of putting a Band-Aid on brain cancer. They are surface treatments that allow us to assume the deeper problem is handled. Morals are not good news. In the wrong hands, they are the enemy of the cross. This is why the ongoing exposure to the gospel is so essential for those of us who are so familiar with it.

We forget sometimes that Jesus's primary audience was composed of really moral people. Professional moralists and religionists, in fact. They were not primarily immoral people. Still, good behavior was the real problem with Jesus's audience. It masked their true condition. As in the religiously overt Southern United States, everyone was saved.

Jesus likened them to actors pulling off flawless impersonations of godly people.

> Woe to you, scribes and Pharisees, hypocrites! For you are like whitewashed tombs which on the outside appear beautiful, but inside they are full of dead men's bones and all uncleanness. So you, too, outwardly appear righteous to men, but inwardly you are full of hypocrisy and lawlessness (Matthew 23:27-28).

This too is counterintuitive. They needed to repent of their personal goodness and high moral standards, not their depraved lifestyles. Jesus was saving them from a trust in their relative goodness, not from their badness. In a real sense, their goodness was their badness. Jesus was calling them to acknowledge and repent of this very reality. They were just like us. Church people. Bible-believing people. Those who have deep convictions about God, hold tightly to the corpus of truth, and live very decent lives. Jesus was ripping the lid off the assumption that had grown around their devotion to God. You can't miss this in Jesus's message.

> Do not think that I came to abolish the Law or the Prophets; I did not come to abolish but to fulfill. For truly I say to you, until heaven and earth pass away, not the smallest letter or stroke shall pass away from the Law until all is accomplished (Matthew 5:17-18).

Jesus kicked open the back door of their religiously dense culture and let the truth in. They were whitewashed tombs. For centuries, they had assumed they were related to God because they were related to Abraham. John the Baptist confronted the religious leaders on this very defect in their thinking.

> When he saw many of the Pharisees and Sadducees coming for baptism, he said to them, "You brood of vipers, who warned you to flee from the wrath to come? Therefore bear fruit in keeping with repentance; and do not suppose that you can say to yourselves, 'We have Abraham for our

father'; for I say to you, that from these stones God is able
to raise up children to Abraham. The axe is already laid at
the root of the trees; every tree that does not bear good fruit
is cut down and thrown into the fire" (Matthew 3:7-10).

If Jesus's message had been "be good and moral," these men
would have no need to change anything about their lives. They were
already there. They would have seen no need for Christ or His cross.
They would have been like the passenger on the plane that Schaeffer
described. This is exactly why Jesus's message reached beyond morality to the heart condition that lay underneath. Why else would Jesus
say what He did?

> He was reclining at the table in [Levi's] house, and many
> tax-gatherers and sinners were dining with Jesus and His
> disciples; for there were many of them, and they were fol-
> lowing Him. When the scribes of the Pharisees saw that He
> was eating with the sinners and tax collectors, they began
> saying to His disciples, "Why is He eating and drinking
> with tax collectors and sinners?" And hearing this, Jesus
> said to them, "It is not those who are healthy who need a
> physician, but those who are sick; I did not come to call the
> righteous, but sinners" (Mark 2:15-17).

He was warning them not to assume that their morality, quality of life, and biblical knowledge had anything to do with a proper
standing before God. They were just as sick and in need of grace as
common whores. This is exactly why Jesus's message sent shrapnel
through His culture. The message of salvation by grace was disruptive
to the core. You have to see it this way to read Jesus rightly. We too
often misunderstand His message as one of moral reform and personal improvement. As if Jesus were singling out the nonreligious. It
was anything but.

For example. How often have we heard the Beatitudes offered
as platitudes about deeper spirituality? That's the typical spin on
them. In reality they are laser-guided bombs aimed at the long-held

assumptions of a religious culture. Basically, they were intended to disrupt the religious. Read them again.

> Blessed are the poor in spirit, for theirs is the kingdom of heaven.
> Blessed are those who mourn, for they shall be comforted.
> Blessed are the gentle, for they shall inherit the earth.
> Blessed are those who hunger and thirst for righteousness, for they shall be satisfied.
> Blessed are the merciful, for they shall receive mercy.
> Blessed are the pure in heart, for they shall see God.
> Blessed are the peacemakers, for they shall be called sons of God (Matthew 5:3-9).

In each case, Jesus was dismantling long-held convictions that blinded church people from their need for grace. Jesus pulled apart these assumptions piece by piece. The beatitudes are profoundly counterintuitive. In the culture's perspective, the poor in spirit didn't inherit the kingdom of heaven; the self-righteous did—the ones who had their lives together. Satisfaction was available to those who performed best, not to those who hungered and thirsted for righteousness. The Beatitudes are a delicate-sounding introduction to His redundant Sermon on the Mount, which sent shock waves all over Palestine. It gets more disruptive the further you venture into it. Eventually Jesus is taking one misguided assumption after another head-on. "You have heard it said...but I say to you." Early on He makes the problem clear. "Beware of practicing your righteousness before men to be noticed by them; otherwise you have no reward with your Father who is in heaven" (Matthew 6:1).

The core of His message was aimed at people who knew the truth. They had been raised memorizing entire sections of the Bible. They were so very near the truth and so very far away from it at the same time. This is our greatest danger. We are too familiar with the gospel. We are too comfortable around the cross. We too easily lose the awe-inspiring wonder of Calvary. We assume it's for others and not for us. We are knowledgeable, decent, and well-behaved but seemingly unbroken in the presence of Jesus. Somehow we conservatives are under the impression that making a big deal about Jesus is optional or even inappropriate. It is neither.

It's Okay to Be Excited About Jesus, Right?

About the same time Joe showed up in my life, I was working through the Gospel of Matthew. I had faithfully preached through the book for more than two years and nearly missed the point. The account of a woman anointing Jesus's feet finally brought everything into focus. This broken woman nailed my heart to the wall. Her extravagant devotion to Jesus blasted a hole in all my well-informed neglect. Like all those men who were present when she had the presence of mind to do what she did, I had forgotten to love and adore Jesus. I too had missed Him. Like the Twelve, I'd been the guy quarrelling over pocket change while missing the unbelievable treasure sitting in front of me. After all these years of educating myself and others about Jesus, I forgot to worship and praise Him for His love. Years later, Peter, who was present when this event went down, exhorted us not to make the same mistake he did.

> Though you have not seen Him, you love Him, and though you do not see Him now, but believe in Him, you greatly rejoice with joy inexpressible and full of glory, obtaining as the outcome of your faith the salvation of your souls (1 Peter 1:8-9).

As it turns out, it's okay to make a big deal about Jesus.

> Now when Jesus was in Bethany, at the home of Simon the leper, a woman came to Him with an alabaster vial of very costly perfume, and she poured it upon His head as He reclined at the table (Matthew 26:6-7).

I can only imagine how uncomfortable she made everyone in attendance. This would have been shocking behavior. This was unsuitable for church and disruptive to the extreme. She stepped on nearly every taboo and knocked over every tradition in existence to get to Jesus. This type of display would have been highly controversial for anyone, but a woman doing it pushed the whole scene over the top. It was beyond scandalous. Not surprisingly, it angered every conservative church person present.

> But the disciples were indignant when they saw this, and said, "Why this waste? For this perfume might have been sold for a high price and the money given to the poor" (verses 8-9).

The disciples completely missed it. They had been missing it for months. But *it* had been there the entire time. So close yet so far. At this moment, they were upset about meeting all the expenses associated with Jesus's ministry and forgot Jesus's true mission in the process. But she (along with countless other atypical characters in the Bible) did not miss it. She got it. And in the biggest way.

"Waste" is the dominant word in this passage. It leaps off the page. A simple symbol can sum up the entirety of our perspective. One person's waste is another person's worship. I suppose it all depends on the one on whom you're wasting it. What they saw as waste, she considered an inadequate sacrifice. They were unwilling to go to such lengths to demonstrate their love and gratitude for Christ. To do so was beneath them. They didn't realize that their rebuke revealed their true estimation of Jesus Christ, just as we don't realize that our lack of brokenness around such amazing biblical facts reveals ours. Jesus rebuked the disciples and us.

> But Jesus, aware of this, said to them, "Why do you bother the woman? For she has done a good deed to Me. For you always have the poor with you; but you do not always have Me" (verses 10-11).

Not surprisingly, the very behavior that offended everyone else in attendance pleased Jesus. That happened a lot. What others saw as careless, Jesus called good. According to Jesus, her level of sacrifice and devotion was appropriately scandalous. All this time with Jesus, these men had failed to see Him for who He was. He had been telling them all along what He came to do for them, but it never occurred to them to worship Him for it.

> He warned the disciples that they should tell no one that He was the Christ.
>
> From that time Jesus began to show His disciples that He must go to Jerusalem, and suffer many things from the elders and chief priests and scribes, and be killed, and be raised up on the third day. Peter took Him aside and began to rebuke Him, saying, "God forbid it, Lord! This shall never happen to You" (Matthew 16:20-22).

Jesus was clutter. That was me. I had forgotten to worship my Savior. I, too, had failed to kiss the feet of the one who gave Himself for me. This type of adoration was above me. I eventually realized I couldn't possibly overstate a sincere adoration of the person and work of Christ. That's impossible. But I could easily forget to demonstrate it at all.

There are so many things to learn from this humble woman's devotion to Christ. She shames me on every level.

- Her worship was a spontaneous and natural expression of love for Christ. It spills out of her heart. My worship of Christ most often begins promptly at nine every Sunday morning.

- Her worship is uninhibited. It does not stop to concern itself with what men may think. Mine is safely confined within the bounds of respectability.

- Her worship was unflinchingly sacrificial. Mine hesitates.

- Her worship was bold and defiant. The others in the room immediately knew how deeply she believed in Jesus. At times, you have to look hard at my life to see an ounce of pure devotion.

But don't miss what drew this praise from her heart. It wasn't simply Jesus. It was His substitutionary life and death that broke her heart and snapped her vial of perfume. It was His sacrifice for sinners. It was the thing about Him that made Him different from every other person.

> For when she poured this perfume on My body, she did it to prepare Me for burial. Truly I say to you, wherever this gospel is preached in the whole world, what this woman has done will also be spoken of in memory of her (Matthew 26:12-13).

She got it. Her worship put the sacrificial work of Christ on display. The gospel had gripped her heart. Even if no one else was going to thank Him or worship Him for what He was about to do, she would. It wasn't simply Jesus she caused a scene over. It was what Jesus would do for her in a few short days. Jesus would carry her burden on His own back up a hill and die. It was the cross. Jesus makes this plain in His response. The extraordinary grace of God in the substitutionary death of Christ had provoked this humble worship. It always does.

 **Part 2**

The Bible

Something so much greater is underway in these sacred pages. These events were not intended to be spiritualized into oblivion and dissected as lessons about raising kids or starting businesses. They are intended to be marveled at by God's people. We stand and point at what God has done. They are each a link in a chain of redemptive history that moves from Genesis to Revelation. They're not isolated at all. They're amazing demonstrations of the divine continuity of God's power. They are each the commitment of a Holy God to keep His promises and honor His holy name among men. Our response to the individual incidents should be, "Look how God used this to get us to Jesus," not "Look how this relates to my longing for significance."

Searching for the
Moral of the Story

Behold, the word of the LORD came to him, saying, "This man will not be your heir; but one who will come forth from your own body, he shall be your heir." And He took him outside and said, "Now look toward the heavens, and count the stars, if you are able to count them." And He said to him, "So shall your descendants be." Then he believed in the LORD; and He reckoned it to him as righteousness.

GENESIS 15:4-6

When I consider Your heavens, the work of Your fingers,
The moon and the stars, which You have ordained;
What is man that You take thought of him,
And the son of man that You care for him?

PSALM 8:3-4

Noah's Raindrop

The suburban church is constantly revising the Bible's message, and that is a major reason why the modern Christian in America has no real idea what the Bible is all about. Most view it as a handbook for one's spiritual life or a guide to finding God's will. But—you might want to sit down for this—it's neither. There's a much bigger story than *us*. At best, we are the collateral damage of God's grace.

The Bible is the breathtaking account of what God has done, what

He is doing, and what He will finally finish on this planet. Unfortunately, you hardly ever hear the real story. The Bible can't get a word in edgewise. The real story is gagged and bound by our self-absorption. We shove our need for personal value down the Bible's throat. Nearly every passage we touch somehow magically turns to *us*. This is such a shame. The real story is so amazing.

The things we've done with the Bible over the years are comical. Our modern edits are beyond creative. Our go-to move is to read our suburban message into the lives of Old Testament characters and events. We have our way with these descriptive sections of the Bible. As we do, we assume we know exactly what was going through the ancient people's minds. We know beyond a doubt the specific personal lesson God intended. Of course, it always happens to be the same lesson we're currently learning in our own lives. It's uncanny.

We use a specific formula to reroute the Bible's plotline. We've been working it for years. If you stick to it, you can blow people's minds with principles they've never seen in the Bible. Usually, this is because they're not actually in there. We're more or less spinning Christian yarns. There's a rhythm to it. Once you find it, amazing things happen. Let me see if I can demonstrate. I'll talk you through the specific steps of the suburban interpretive model. (Spoiler alert! These are trade secrets. This will be awesome.)

First, choose a biblical story. For our purposes I've selected the story of Noah and the ark. Everyone knows the story of Noah. There's a lot to work with here.

> They went into the ark to Noah, by twos of all flesh in which was the breath of life. Those that entered, male and female of all flesh, entered as God had commanded him; and the LORD closed it behind him.
>
> Then the flood came upon the earth for forty days; and the water increased and lifted up the ark, so that it rose above the earth. The water prevailed and increased greatly upon the earth; and the ark floated on the surface of the water. The water prevailed more and more upon the earth, so that

all the high mountains everywhere under the heavens were covered (Genesis 7:15-19).

Second, find an implied and relatively justifiable nuance in this familiar story. What we're trying to do is extract a device that will serve as the central image of the lesson we want to communicate. We'll use it to motivate the listener.

Make sure to stay away from any explicit point in the text, or you'll be limited to what the Bible says. In the long run, this will only hinder our ability to embellish the story. At this point I'd recommend you set your Bible aside. No need confusing ourselves with the facts. Remember, the actual point of the biblical story may conflict with what we're saying or with what the modern audience wants to hear.

Now, to find what we're looking for, all you need to do is put yourself in the moment. You are Noah. Simply imagine the event happening as if you were there. You might want to close your eyes and visualize. Okay, good. You can smell the wood. You can hear the animals. You're counting by twos. You're standing beside the ark. Look around. What's happening? (You are Noah and Noah is you.)

We know Noah was building the boat per God's instructions. We also know it rained. And it rained for 40 days and 40 nights. Excellent. You're on to something here. Focus on the rain. You might be inclined to pass over the rain at first. After all, it's such an obvious point. But don't. Trust me, everything you're looking for is in the rain. You're Noah standing out in the rain. You can hear it. You can smell it. You can feel it. Think. Put yourself in the very second it began to rain. *And there it is.* Can't you see it? It's obvious—the first raindrop that ever fell to earth. We'll call it Noah's Raindrop. How awesome is that? Logically, there had to be a first raindrop. It had never rained before. This idea has serious potential. It pops off the page.

Third, now that you've isolated the specific concept, all you need to do is adjust it to fit suburban Christians and apply it. Suburban Christians are our target audience. Experts suggest it's good to assign your target audience an identity. This way you can have someone specific in mind as you apply the story. (You might want to refer to Barna Research for help on this.) We'll call him Joe Suburb.

Now, what does the first raindrop communicate to Joe Suburb? Or even better, what does Joe need the raindrop to communicate? Since the Bible has nothing at all to say about the first raindrop, your options are limitless. If I were you I'd avoid the totality of precipitation found in this event. This will only lead to extremely negative themes.

As you start reflecting, you may want to play the soundtrack to *Braveheart* or another epic movie. It helps set the mood. Okay, back to the brainstorming. This is where it gets fun and the ideas really start flowing. Don't be concerned about writer's block. There's plenty here to work with. You remember the brief mention of a guy named Jabez in the Bible? An entire industry grew up around this story. Seriously, someone pulled a rabbit out of that passage. "Expand Your Territory." That's a once-in-a-lifetime find, but your passage is loaded with material as well. So you're good to go.

What does a raindrop tell us about *us*? How do we want to apply it? You don't need to look far for an answer. There's one popular application that never disappoints. It works every time—*a yearning for significance.* We know that modern Christians are obsessive about purpose and aims in life. We want to know that our life has consequence. If it doesn't, we want to believe it can. After all, this is what becoming a Christian is all about. So if I were you, I'd stay right here. It's a sweet spot in the modern church. Create the itch of significance and then scratch it with loosely referenced Bible stories. You can't go wrong.

Okay. Now on to the fourth step. Let's turn this idea into a fully developed motivational message about personal significance. This shouldn't be too hard. Let's think through it. That first raindrop was the most important raindrop ever to fall to earth. Ultimately, it led to a worldwide flood. But, that's not important for our purposes. We're not asking why was there a flood, but how that raindrop was important to Noah. How did it inspire him? How did it help him overcome his lack of significance?

If I'm Noah, that raindrop changed everything. I would have been mulling over the idea of a flooded earth for days. I would have been laboring with hammers and nails, building something I did not completely understand—like when we work on parts of projects at work without being given the total vision. Is there anything more frustrating? We struggle for motivation when we aren't able to see the greater vision.

Like us, Noah had a purpose, but he hadn't realized how it fit into the overall scheme of things. Noah was accomplishing something great but had no awareness of how great it was. After all, he had never seen rain. He was merely driving nails with little clarity about what his life meant. Our lives can be just as monotonous as Noah's. (Note the effortless transition to us.) Lots of doing and being, but nothing of consequence to show for it. Like driving nails into gopher wood. Until…that first raindrop. This moment was the moment when the world opened up to Noah. From here we can extrapolate all kinds of ways it affected him. This will flat preach.

Fifth, flesh this message out to a broader audience. In the industry, we call this crafting the message. It might be helpful to write a brief and inspirational paragraph, which might go on the back of a book jacket. Something that would grab the attention of a potential reader. Let me take a shot.

> Have you ever considered the first raindrop that fell to earth? That first raindrop to hit Noah's face? Noah's raindrop. You need to. We all need to. That one little drop of water began a tidal wave in one small life. It changed the course of history. There would be countless raindrops for 40 days and 40 nights, but it was that first splash on Noah's face that changed his life forever and inspired him to be the man God had called him to be. Noah would never forget it. In the precise moment Noah and his raindrop collided, it all became clear. He understood exactly what God had

called him to. That was more than rain falling from the sky on that day…

Wait for it…

…it was inspiration falling from the presence of God. That raindrop spilled from the throne of God. God has a raindrop for you.

Sixth, let's work on the visual. There are unending options with raindrops. Off the top of my head I imagine a close-up picture of a raindrop. It's set against a blue sky in the background. In the raindrop there are reflections of Noah, animals, and the ark. Underneath the massive raindrop are your title and a tagline:

NOAH'S RAINDROP:
HOW PURPOSE FALLS FROM THE PRESENCE OF GOD
INTO YOUR WORLD
Rain is coming.

A series of video shorts would also be powerful. We could follow the raindrop as it starts as a tear from the eye of God and falls to earth. The camera traces its descent through the various layers of the atmosphere until it pierces the cloudbanks and explodes onto Noah's cheek. Of course, that crucial moment is captured in super slow mo. Noah's face is turned upward; he has a distant look in his eyes. The scene is capped off with a massive explosion of thunder. No doubt this is how it sounded to the angels in heaven.

Beyond this, there are posters, raindrop study Bibles, raindrop earrings for teenage girls, journals, a low-production movie and, of course, Noah's Raindrop Bottled Water. Now, how easy was that? And remember, all this from something that's not even mentioned in the story itself. Amazing. I should submit a book proposal. Seriously, this would sell.

Putting Words in God's Mouth

I was standing in the Southern Hemisphere, staring up at the night sky with the Southern Cross suspended right above me. It was my first time to see this constellation. It can't be seen from where I normally stand. The night was on fire in central Tanzania. Stars without number against a velvet blackness were untouched by the intrusive lights of progress. This was night as it was intended. The depth of space was drawing out my smallness. Silence enveloped me.

The amateur astronomer standing next to me broke the worship and asked, "You see that massive cloudlike band of stars across the sky?" Her finger swung over us as she traced the expanse to the horizon at our backs. It did seem cloudlike. "That's the Milky Way. We're somewhere in that." My mind was immediately blown to pieces by the consequence of her subtle observation. I was gazing out at something I was in.

Never have words so unintentionally summed up the consequence of me. Looking upward I composed a single line of praise: "I am so insignificant." I'm not sure if the sky seemed greater due to my insignificance or if I seemed more insignificant due to the sky's greatness. Either way, the result was the same. I was humbled but strangely grateful for the effect. It sized me up. Somewhere down those infinite corridors of numberless stars and galaxies stands a single speck of a man gazing up at a billion reasons why God is great. There are stars without number out there. God knows them each by name. This mind-blowing observation was eventually overshadowed by a much greater one—He also knows mine. How's that even possible? Who am I that God would care for me? Apparently, God is a lover of specks.

I was born on March 4, 1970. There's no way to describe how grateful I am for this date in history. Not merely because it's when I was born, but because of where the date lies on the calendar of human history. An unbelievably gracious God determined I would arrive on the side of history that looks back at death's defeat. The first breath my infant lungs took in was filled with the dust of an empty tomb stirred by the resurrection of Jesus Christ. I came to life at a point in God's redemptive expanse where the cross dominates both horizons of history. I can trace it over my life. I can see all that God has done and will do from where I stand. It is breathtaking.

Looking into the pages of the Bible is very much like pointing out at a galaxy that possesses us. When we read the Bible's epoch of redemption, we're gazing out at something we are in. It's hard to fathom how great this reality is, but we must try if we are to get the story right. From where we stand (in these brief years we call a life) we can point to the beginning of time in Genesis and trace God's grace as it runs over us toward its consummation at the end of time in Revelation. We are somewhere in this amazing unfolding. We're in that. We were among those stars promised to Abraham ages ago. In the pages of biblical history we gaze on that which possesses us. We are watching the unfolding of the promise.

The Bible is not ancient history stagnant on a page. It is not spiritual advice. It is not about what goes on inside us. It is about what went on outside us. It is the record of redemption. It is the unfolding of everything we know. It is what God has done, is doing, and will bring to pass. It is the chronicle of God's love on a rampage through human history, overcoming everything in its path, taking down sinners with grace, and bringing about a serpent-crushing event in the cross of Christ. We are in that.

We have no idea of the privilege of where we stand as New Testament believers. Our vantage point is the envy of ancient prophets and countless Old Testament saints now staring down from heaven. They waited so long to witness the events we now take for granted. They lived and died in anticipation. They would have given anything to stand in the hemisphere of the resurrection, breathe in its air, and see what we see.

> As to this salvation, the prophets who prophesied of the grace that would come to you made careful searches and inquiries, seeking to know what person or time the Spirit of Christ within them was indicating as He predicted the sufferings of Christ and the glories to follow. It was revealed to them that they were not serving themselves, but you, in these things which now have been announced to you through those who preached the gospel to you by the Holy

Spirit sent from heaven—things into which angels long to look (1 Peter 1:10-12).

How frustrated they must be as they watch modern Christians obsess about lesser things. We spend all our time gazing inward and not out at the amazing thing God has done for sinners. We're missing the edge-of-your-seat thrill ride of redemptive history found on the pages of Scripture. Angels are bent over in awe of the story unfolding down here, and we're too preoccupied with our own story to notice. As we look for the moral of the story, the story passes us by.

Most Christians would be shocked to realize how often they misread the Bible and subtly deny its divine authority. We usually reserve this type of criticism for liberals, but this is true even for those who hold the Bible in highest regard. The difference between the two groups is only slight. They each make it something it's not. One group dismisses the supernatural origin and contents, seeking to make it an ordinary book. The other group acknowledges its supernatural origin and contents but treats it like an ordinary book. Think this is going too far?

Do we not generally view the Bible as a handbook of principles for life or a basic moral guide or a manual for self-improvement? This approach is only somewhat removed from liberal theology. Liberal theology edits entire sections out of the Bible. Popular Christianity edits entire meanings into it. Anytime we reduce the Bible down to ethics, we're no different from those who think the Bible is a myth.

Fact is, suburban Christianity has been coming up with the wrong story from the same book for a long time. It's possible some Christians who love the Word of God very deeply have missed its point entirely. There's a much greater story in the Bible than the realization of your life's purpose. You and I are a small part of something that possesses us. If "small" seems harsh, you've missed the point of what you've been reading. You've been standing in the wrong hemisphere staring out at the wrong object. When you read it rightly, "small" makes sense. In fact, "small" makes you strangely grateful for what you see.

I hate to disappoint you, but the Bible is not about you. Specifically, it was not written to improve the quality of your daily existence
(in the way you think.) The Bible is not a story of God determining
in eternity past to send His Son to earth to create a more satisfactory
existence for you. This is usually where we take the story. We are seriously self-absorbed. Who else could take the unbelievable episode of
Moses and the burning bush and bend it back toward our everyday
experience? Can't you see the angels rolling their eyes? Your life and
happiness are not adequate points of reference for the scope of what
God has done and is doing. Neither are mine. It's bigger than you and
me. We are watching as redemption comes to pass on the pages of
Scripture, one unbelievable event after another, eventually leading to
Christ. Each page rumbles with anticipation. When you see it from
here, the Bible opens up in ways you've never imagined. It takes off.

Unfortunately, we've been conditioned to read ourselves onto the
pages and into the events of Scripture. We don't even realize we're
doing it. What's the first question we ask of the Bible in our personal
reading times or church services? "How is this relevant to me?" This is
the wrong question entirely. No question could push us further from
the real story. It's very much like walking out into the night sky and
assuming all the stars showed up to look at us. When we approach
the Bible this way, we can't help but read it as if we're the center of
the biblical universe and all of its history revolves around us. When
everything is read through the lens of self, self-improvement, and self-
contentment, we're destined to miss the point. But this is what we
always do. Is it any wonder most Christians—even those who care
deeply about the Word of God—are unable to put it all together?

Usually, biblical stories are approached as a set of isolated events
with no connection to each other or to the greater redemptive plotline of the Bible. Without the real story, the events of the Bible
become merely parables for better living, moral platitudes, character studies, or whatever else we can come up with. In the absence of
a greater plot this is all we have. Over the years popular Christianity has practically rewritten the Bible. Our version of various events
reads more like a fairy tale than God's story.

- Eve's decision to eat of the fruit and the subsequent disintegration of humanity becomes a lesson on the effects of negligent leadership and an absentee husband.

- Cain's homicidal rage becomes a lesson on avoiding sibling rivalry.

- Abraham's attempted sacrifice of his only son becomes a lesson in parenting.

- Moses before a burning bush becomes a prototype for decision making.

- Gideon becomes an example of how to determine the will of God.

- The prayer of Jabez becomes a lesson about expanding our personal influence.

- David's encounter with the fighting champion of a hostile nation becomes a lesson in overcoming our greatest personal challenges ("giants").

- Jonah, a prophet miraculously swallowed by a fish and vomited out on a specific shoreline, becomes an example of the futility of resisting God's purpose in your life.

- A young unnamed paralytic dropped through a roof at the feet of Jesus by four men becomes a lesson on the value of friendship.

None of these interpretations are remotely close to the real point of the events themselves. We've told them wrong. You may think I'm crazy, but stick with me. I used to approach the Bible the same way. I totally missed it. Or to be more specific, I missed the point. *All these events and people lead us to the person of Jesus.* It's about Jesus.

The lessons we typically draw out of the biblical stories are secondary observations at best. Usually this is because it's all we know to do with them. Fact is, the same sort of life lessons could be derived from any contemporary biography or history. The meanings and applications we've given these events have nothing at all to do with what's going on in the true story. Our approach is about the same as looking for stock tips in the sonnets of Shakespeare. This oversight is so very tragic.

Something so much greater is underway in these sacred pages. These events were not intended to be spiritualized into oblivion and dissected as lessons about raising kids or starting businesses. They are intended to be marveled at by God's people. We stand and point at what God has done. They are each a link in a chain of redemptive history that moves from Genesis to Revelation. They're not isolated at all. They're amazing demonstrations of the divine continuity of God's power. They are each the commitment of a holy God to keep His promises and honor His holy name among men. Our response to the individual incidents should be, "Look how God used this to get us to Jesus," not "Look how this relates to my longing for significance."

We've lost the main story line that pulls all the pieces together and gives them a consistent meaning, so we essentially take what's available and make up a story. What we've come up with in evangelicalism is a bit like *Little House on the Prairie*. (Didn't Michael Landon bear a strange resemblance to King David?) The Bible is now the epic tale of trials and triumph on the frontier of a long-ago land. It is no longer about what God has been doing for man and is more about what humanity has done to impress God. We approach it more as a collection of fables that indirectly offer principles for life. The Bible is no longer about how God went about saving humanity from the brink of desolation. The Bible is more the account of how God occasionally stopped to applaud the faith of a few exceptional people. It's less about what He has done. It's almost exclusively what we can do if we learn from the lives of heroic figures in God's Word.

We do the weirdest things to the Bible in the absence of the cohesive theme. No other book is treated so recklessly by people who honor that same book so greatly. Among our favorite rewrites are character sketches. We like to examine the lives of Old Testament saints—triumphs and tragedies alike—and offer various patterns for living. Almost everyone assumes this is the very reason the Old

Testament saints show up in the biblical record. Abraham, Joseph, Moses, Joshua, Gideon, and Deborah have all come to represent examples to live by (or not to). What else could be the reason for the focus on their lives? Therefore we mine them for spiritual and moral principles. Sermons are preached and books are written about their lives and offered as blueprints for daily life, success in business, or practical decision-making skills.

Every Sunday kids sit in Sunday school classes, look at flannel boards or snip at construction paper with safety scissors, and learn how these ancient figures are examples of faithfulness or failure. The consistent message is, be like them and life will work out better. Or don't be like them and life will work out better. Work harder, make good decisions, and stay out of trouble like Joseph, and God will bless you.

When these same kids reach their early twenties, struggle with real life, and fail to reach Joseph's moral high ground, they despair. They can't do it. Joseph was exceptional. They get angry with God when life does not work out according to the coloring pages. Eventually they find Christianity irrelevant and powerless to save them, and they walk away.

They're exactly right—Joseph *is* powerless to save them. We're creating angry moralists, setting them up for failure, and blaming it on the Bible. Tragically, the one message that actually could save them from their failure was before us in the story of Joseph the entire time. We failed to mention it. Families would run from our children's programs if parents knew the effect our Bible lessons are having on their kids.

This approach to understanding this amazing book could not push us further from the real message and central character of the Bible. I know this sounds ridiculous to most of us and maybe even sacrilegious to some, but it should be obvious. The Bible is about Jesus, not Moses or any other biblical figure. The point of Moses is not Moses, but the one to whom Moses points. The Bible explicitly argues this very thing.

Therefore, holy brethren, partakers of a heavenly calling, consider Jesus, the Apostle and High Priest of our confession; He was faithful to Him who appointed Him, as Moses also was in all His house. For He has been counted worthy of more glory than Moses, by just so much as the builder of the house has more honor than the house. For every house is built by someone, but the builder of all things is God. Now Moses was faithful in all His house as a servant, for a testimony of those things which were to be spoken later; but Christ was faithful as a Son over His house—whose house we are, if we hold fast our confidence and the boast of our hope firm until the end (Hebrews 3:1-6).

Bill Versus Abraham

In contrast, the way we've been taught to understand the Bible runs directly across the grain of the Bible's own point. David is not in the Bible so you could learn about David. Is it okay to learn from the examples of biblical characters? On a certain level, yes. Some of them do serve as *types* of Christ. But the intended parallel to Jesus is not their impeccable quality or individual achievements. Their personal biography is not the purpose for their existence. The existence of someone greater is the purpose for their existence. They all point to Christ in one way or another. They all point to the desperate need for Christ all humans share.

If the exceptional character of faithful people is the point of the Bible, I could just as legitimately write a study on the life of some exceptional Christian in my life. Why can't we also pattern our lives after good people we know? I know some very faithful people. In fact, I'd go on record to say they're more faithful than Abraham or David. Unlike Abraham, they've never given up their wives to the pimp down the street to save their hide. Unlike David, they've never committed adultery, fathered a bastard child, and attempted to cover it up by murdering a devoted upper-level official in the army. Morally speaking, Abraham and David look like chumps compared to some people I know.

Now that I think about it, I could extract some incredible life lessons from many of my friends' existence. What if I did just that? What if I wrote a study on the life of some person I respect, passed it out to our people, and led a 13-week class on it in our church? Let's do it. We'll call him Bill. Here are some of the lessons.

- Bill's background and how it affected his decisions later in life.

- The providence of God in Bill's experience.

- Bill's greatest failures and the contributing factors.

- Bill's triumph and how he trusted God in hard times.

What do you think would happen if I did this? I'd lose my job. My people would freak! Bill would freak! They would consider it blasphemous. Why? Because I chose to focus on a fallen and finite human being and not Jesus Christ, the incarnate Son of God. Bill is a human being. Bill is a sinner who needs Jesus as much as I do. Bill is just as much in need of saving as I am. Bill cannot save me. Jesus came into this world because no human being was capable of saving anyone.

Obviously, my idea about Bill sounds absurd, right? Exactly! But this is what we do. We focus our faith and attention on other broken human beings and not on Jesus or what God did in Jesus.

But someone will object, "Abraham is a biblical character. Bill is not a biblical character." Here's the deal. The fact that Abraham appears in the Bible does not make him divine or sacred. He's a human being like any other human being. Both Abraham and Bill are fallen human beings. Although separated by centuries, they are the same guy. They both need someone outside of themselves to save them. They're both pointing out at something that possesses and saves them, albeit from different dates on the calendar and from different sides of the tomb. They are both relatively insignificant in the scheme of things. Specks under the same expanse of God's redemption. Jesus agreed with this estimation of Abraham.

> The Jews said to Him…"Surely You are not greater than our father Abraham, who died? The prophets died too;

whom do You make Yourself out to be?" Jesus answered, "If I glorify Myself, My glory is nothing; it is My Father who glorifies Me, of whom you say, 'He is our God'; and you have not come to know Him, but I know Him; and if I say that I do not know Him, I will be a liar like you, but I do know Him and keep His word. Your father Abraham rejoiced to see My day, and he saw it and was glad." So the Jews said to Him, "You are not yet fifty years old, and have You seen Abraham?" Jesus said to them, "Truly, truly, I say to you, before Abraham was born, I am." Therefore they picked up stones to throw at Him; but Jesus hid Himself, and went out of the temple (John 8:52-59).

In other words, "Abraham points to Me and not to himself." To focus on Abraham is to miss the message of Abraham's life. Basically, Jesus told the Jewish leaders, "You've missed the point of Abraham. I am the point." They missed the point of the Bible just as we do. Paul, formerly a self-righteous Jew and an expert on all things Abraham, agreed as well.

What then shall we say that Abraham, our forefather according to the flesh, has found? For if Abraham was justified by works, he has something to boast about; but not before God. For what does the Scripture say? "Abraham believed God, and it was credited to him as righteousness." Now to the one who works, his wage is not credited as a favor, but as what is due. But to the one who does not work, but believes in Him who justifies the ungodly, his faith is reckoned as righteousness, just as David also speaks of the blessing on the man to whom God reckons righteousness apart from works:

"Blessed are those whose lawless deeds have been forgiven,
And whose sins have been covered.
Blessed is the man whose sin the Lord will not take into account.

Is this blessing then on the circumcised, or on the uncir-
cumcised also? For we say, "Faith was credited to Abraham
as righteousness"...

For the promise to Abraham or to his descendants that he
would be heir of the world was not through the Law, but
through the righteousness of faith. For if those who are of
the Law are heirs, faith is made void and the promise is nul-
lified; for the Law brings about wrath, but where there is
no law, neither is there violation.

For this reason it is by faith, in order that it may be in accor-
dance with grace, so that the promise will be guaranteed to
all the descendants, not only to those who are of the Law,
but also to those who are of the faith of Abraham, who
is the father of us all, (as it is written, "A father of many
nations have I made you") in the presence of Him whom
he believed, even God, who gives life to the dead and calls
into being that which does not exist. In hope against hope
he believed, so that he might become a father of many
nations according to that which had been spoken, "So shall
your descendants be" (Romans 4:1-9,13-18).

It does not matter that Abraham shows up in specific details of
the Bible's plotline. Ultimately, both Abraham and Bill are included
in the epoch of redemption at different points. They are both in the
Bible, because Bill was among the stars God pointed out to Abraham.
Abraham was included in the stars promised to Abraham. After all,
there is no difference between Abraham and Bill. Abraham is not a
better person than Bill. God could have produced a people out of Bill
just as easily as he did from Abraham. To think otherwise is to deny
a central tenet of the gospel and the main story line of the Bible: "All
have sinned and fall short of the glory of God" (Romans 3:23). We
seem to forget that "all" includes Abraham, Isaac, Jacob, and Bill.

The individual characters in the Bible don't show up because anything about them was particularly significant. In fact, most were chosen because they were insignificant. Significance is reserved for Jesus.

The LORD did not set His love on you nor choose you
because you were more in number than any of the peoples,
for you were the fewest of all peoples, but because the LORD
loved you and kept the oath which He swore to your forefathers, the LORD brought you out by a mighty hand and
redeemed you from the house of slavery, from the hand of
Pharaoh king of Egypt (Deuteronomy 7:7-8).

More importantly, each one of these people points to the universal need for the person of Jesus. Abraham proves that all of us need
someone to save us because Abraham himself needed Jesus as much
as Bill does. Regardless of how faithful Abraham was (and he was not
especially faithful), faith in Abraham will not save anyone. Regardless of how great David's victories were (his failures were greater), he
could not gain the victory over your sin. Regardless of how committed Joseph was (he did not set out to save Egypt and Israel from
famine), he could not deliver us from the plague of our depravity.
Daniel's devotion could not save us from our lack of it.

None of these people could save themselves. They were all los-
ers like the rest of us. Sinful, broken, train wrecks whose bright spots
were the rare exceptions of their lives. It is not their faithfulness, but
the object of their faith that is essential. If you don't see it this way,
you will never get the Bible. You will always think the point is to pattern your life after other sinful people. This creates a desperate loop
of existence. You will always read the potential of your own life into
the story. God chose these people not because they were special, but
because they weren't. They are just like the rest of us. Broken. Abraham is Bill. Accept it.

When the Pharisees approached John the Baptist, they assumed
the unique privilege of being descendants of their man of the mil-
lennium (Abraham). But John sent them packing to the back of the
line with everybody else. Abraham can't do anything for you. Who
cares about Abraham?

When he saw many of the Pharisees and Sadducees coming for baptism, he said to them, "You brood of vipers,

who warned you to flee from the wrath to come? Therefore bear fruit in keeping with repentance; and do not suppose that you can say to yourselves, 'We have Abraham for our father'; for I say to you that from these stones God is able to raise up children to Abraham" (Matthew 3:7-9).

Jesus Himself would have nothing to do with our version of the Bible. When the same band of religious hooligans claimed the same privilege of being in Abraham's family tree, Jesus dismissed them outright. He turned their world on its ear. He made them so mad they tried to kill Him. About as mad as suburban Christians get when you mess with their nursery rhymes.

These figures are important but not because of their character qualities. They are important because of the way God used them to fulfill His promise to save sinners from the condemnation of the planet. Their lives show up in the Bible because God used them to bring His promises to pass. They were in the right place at the right time. Frankly, they could have been anybody.

Someone may interject, "Aren't there exceptions to what you're saying? Wasn't Moses the most humble man on the earth?"

Well, yes he was. And you would be as well if you were the one man on earth who was exposed to God's presence for months at a time. God made him humble. God didn't choose him because he was humble.

"But wasn't David a man after God's own heart?"

Of course, but he was not the only man who had a heart after God's heart. More importantly, David's heart was still deceitfully wicked and corrupt. David was totally depraved just like the rest of humanity.

You know the Hall of Faith in Hebrews 11? That list of saints throughout history who were faithful? The great cloud of witnesses that surround us? We love this passage of Scripture, and rightfully so. It's awesome. But have you noticed that the inclusion of some people on that list makes no sense at all? What in the world is Rahab doing there? She was a pagan harlot. Her life was not characterized by faithfulness. Sure, there was one bright moment, but other than that there's not much good. Or Samson? His life was a disaster, and then he died tragically in a murder-suicide. Seriously, some of the characters on the list don't fit the criteria of faithfulness. They're misfits.

We struggle to make them fit because we miss the point of the chapter. The chapter is not about the faithfulness of the individual people at all. It's about their belief, albeit brief, in the faithfulness of God. Samson regretted his mistakes and believed God in the closing moments of his existence. Some of them were remarkably faithful, but this is not why they make the list. After all, the book of Hebrews is explicitly about the supremacy of Christ over every other potential object of faith. Why would there be a chapter on the faithfulness of people when the entire book is about the faithfulness of Christ? The group of saints that surrounds us is witnessing to the faithfulness of God in Christ. He is the faithful High Priest.

> In these last days [God] has spoken to us in His Son, whom He appointed heir of all things, through whom also He made the world. And He is the radiance of His glory and the exact representation of His nature, and upholds all things by the word of His power. When He had made purification of sins, He sat down at the right hand of the Majesty on high; having become as much better than the angels, as He has inherited a more excellent name than they (Hebrews 1:2-4).

Autographs in Heaven

This is not a story of human potential at all. It's a story of the absence of human potential and what God did to save us from it. It is not primarily a story about what God wants *us* to do and be as people. It is a story about what God did to save us from what we did. It's not a story of how we can live satisfied spiritual lives. It's a story of how God satisfied His own righteous demands. Jesus is not primarily an example to follow. Jesus is a rescuer on a daring mission. He is the God man sent to redeem us from our inability to redeem ourselves. The story is about what happened outside of us that saved us from what was wrong inside of us. If we're not as bad as the Bible says we are, or if we're as good as we say Moses and David are, why did Jesus come and die?

Many of us are thinking heaven will be like Disneyland, where the characters occasionally come out and mingle with the general public. We'll grab the autograph books we bought at heaven's gift shop and wait in line to get their signatures. As they sign our books, we'll say, "Moses, it's an honor to meet you. That thing you did with the plagues was awesome. Thanks so much." But heaven doesn't have a gift shop with merchandise bearing the images of your favorite biblical characters. That theme park is here on earth.

David and the Shot That Couldn't Miss

Consider how some of our traditional understandings of our favorite stories contradict what the Bible is actually saying. Since the story of David and Goliath is the favorite of favorites among our flannel-board translations, we'll start there. Over my lifetime I've heard the story of David and Goliath offered in locker rooms more than on any other occasion. It's the go-to motivational speech of coaches, preachers, and Christians everywhere. Ironically, every time a coach broke it out, I knew we were about to lose. It most often signaled defeat. The coach might as well have said, "You guys don't have a chance. You're much less talented than your opponent. It will be a miracle if you win."

In fact, that would actually have been an accurate application of the story.

What the coach actually said went something like this, "The oddsmakers say you will lose." (You should be humming the theme to *Rocky* at this point.) "But I'm here to tell you if you only believe, your opponents will be delivered into your hands on this day. You will win. Though you are smaller, God is the slayer of giants. You know...like David and Goliath." He would then pray and round off his speech with a good ol' boy call to victory: "Now let's go kick their tails!" That little bit of irony always made me laugh. Then we would bolt from the locker room all charged up and get crushed. In hindsight the lesson was unavoidable—we simply didn't believe enough. This is not much different from the versions of this story offered in pulpits, books, and children's curricula in many conservative churches. We moralize it into oblivion.

One of these days in heaven we're going to sit down with King David and share our take on the Goliath story with him. He is going to laugh his head off. David will do a spit take with his heavenly beverage and then ask, "Are you serious? You mean to tell me there's a movie and everything?" Trust me—he'll have no idea what you are talking about.

Those five stones in the story are not the five opportunities you have to overcome challenges in your life. Your giant is not your mother-in-law (unless she actually is). I've got news for you. David was not going to miss the giant no matter what. He could have turned around backward, blindfolded, tossed the stone over his shoulder left-handed, banking it off of the ark of the covenant, and Goliath would have still gone down. No way he misses. No way Goliath lives. No way David dies. Easiest shot of David's life. Worst day of Goliath's.

The Real Story of David

Here's the real story. Israel wanted a king. They thought it would be politically expedient to have one. They took matters into their own hands, rejecting the direct leadership of their covenant God, and went about finding a monarch and military leader. No more clouds by day and fires by night. Let's get ourselves a real leader like the rest of the nations around here. God obliged and gave them what they wanted. So they chose Saul, *a giant of a man.* The type of man who could face the fighting champions of other nations—like Goliath of the Philistines. We need a warrior. Ironically, it was the concept of human valor that led them to Saul in the first place (1 Samuel 9:1-2). Of course, Saul turned out to be a disaster.

Now, we think Saul's failure was caused by a deficiency in his character. That may be partly true, but it is only a subplot in the bigger story. The real failure was the nation's lack of faith. The people did not trust God to fulfill His promises. They wanted a tangible demonstration of power and authority (as if the sea parting were not enough). In other words, they put their faith in a man and not in God.

Yet God had always fulfilled His promises to His people. He always does. His fulfillment of His promises is in every major event in Israel's history. God was and is now bringing amazing things to pass. They could not see it or simply refused to. Eventually, things get so bad with Saul that the prophet Samuel has his head in his hands on an ash heap somewhere, regretting that he anointed Saul as king.

God comes to Samuel at this point and says, "What are you worried about? I told you what I would do, and I'm doing it. Now, get up." He then sends Samuel into the remote backcountry of Bethlehem (not a coincidence) with anointing oil in hand to a farm, where a farmer named Jesse has eight sons. From these sons God will choose a king who will lead His people into further promise. Of course, when Samuel gets to Bethlehem he's still thinking big and tall. But God warns him, "Do not look at his appearance or at the height of his stature."

He progresses through seven sons, expecting that each will be the king. Eventually, no sons are left. Samuel, who is rather confused at this point, has to ask, "Uh...is this everyone?" Finally Jesse mentions David, as if he had completely forgotten about him. The runt of the family is out in the fields, tending the sheep and practicing his flute (like Mr. Tumnus). To everyone's surprise God says, "This is the one." David is anointed king.

The choice of David is very counterintuitive. Not the choice we would make at all. Different from Saul in every way—which is the point. With David, God will get the glory because God is the obvious source of power in his life. At this point the Spirit descends, officially inaugurating David (remember the baptism scene with Jesus?), and all that remains is the final transfer of power.

The very next episode is Goliath. You know the story. The Philistines amassed their armies on the plains of Canaan, seeking to occupy the territory of the tribe of Judah—a land grab concerning a piece of property God had promised to His people. Once both armies were assembled, the Philistines sent out their fighting champion, Goliath. Winner takes all. If Israel's champion prevailed, the Philistines would be their servants. If the Philistines' champion won, Israel would be theirs. This way mass casualties could be avoided. It was like a duel. Of course, if Israel lost, the real damage would be to the glory of God's name. To be defeated by a pagan nation would shame the name of Jehovah. Needless to say, a lot was at stake. More than we actually realize.

Eventually, David shows up with box lunches for his older brothers. When he hears the Philistines taunting Israel and their fighting champion blaspheming God, David goes ballistic. "No one talks about my God this way." Israel's own fighting champion (Saul) refused to act, so David decides to take matters into his own hands. "I've got this." Where do you suppose such boldness came from? Did I mention the part where the Spirit of God descended on David? David is acting as a king should act. David refuses the official uniform and picks up five stones instead. The number is a clear indication of David's trust in his own skills. Then there is an exchange between warriors.

> The Philistine said to David, "Am I a dog, that you come to me with sticks?" And the Philistine cursed David by his gods. The Philistine also said to David, "Come to me, and I will give your flesh to the birds of the sky and the beasts of the field." Then David said to the Philistine, "You come to me with a sword, a spear, and a javelin, but I come to you in the name of the LORD of hosts, the God of the armies of Israel, whom you have taunted. This day the LORD will deliver you up into my hands, and I will strike you down and remove your head from you. And I will give the dead bodies of the army of the Philistines this day to the birds

of the sky and the wild beasts of the earth, that all the earth may know that there is a God in Israel, and that all this assembly may know that the LORD does not deliver by sword or by spear; for the battle is the LORD's and He will give you into our hands."

Then it happened when the Philistine rose and came and drew near to meet David, that David ran quickly toward the battle line to meet the Philistine. And David put his hand into his bag and took from it a stone and slung it, and struck the Philistine on his forehead. And the stone sank into his forehead, so that he fell on his face to the ground. Thus David prevailed over the Philistine with a sling and a stone, and he struck the Philistine and killed him; but there was no sword in David's hand (1 Samuel 17:43-50).

Round and round the sling goes. Down goes Goliath. As was the tradition of the time, David lops off his opponent's head (call it a trophy) and offers a victory speech. A party ensues. Everyone starts heralding the bravery of David.

But there's no way David loses this battle. Not because he was a great shot or was a man after God's own heart, not because he was handsome or wrote theologically dense poetry, and not because he was a better person than Saul. After all, according to the gospel, David isn't better than Saul.

The victory here had nothing to do with David per se. The victory isn't really the defeat of Goliath. It's all pretty simple, really. It had to do with the promises of God. God had anointed David as king. David had not yet assumed office, so the promise had not yet been fulfilled. Literally, he could not die. God had promised something that was still in the future. Goliath didn't realize that the whole thing was rigged. He was dead before the stone ever left David's hands.

But Goliath going down is not even the amazing part of the story. It's not really the story at all. It's only part of it. What's amazing is that *the stone and our salvation are inextricably linked.* In ways that boggle the mind, Goliath's defeat brought my salvation to pass. Think about it. Long ago God promised to crush the head of the serpent and restore all things. The events that would bring this scene onto the stage of biblical history began to unfold immediately following the fall of mankind. God promised to Abraham that One would come through whom all things would be accomplished. As the story unfolds, we realize this One would come through David's line. God promised to David that from his offspring would emerge the King of kings and Lord of lords. This future King would put His heel on the serpent's head. The Lord would win a battle over sin that David could never win.

Literally, if David dies on the field of battle, mankind is doomed. My heart is glued to the page as I watch a gracious God cause the most amazing things to happen in order that sinners may be delivered from a reality greater than pagan giants. The story of David and Goliath is epic on a scale we never really consider. It all comes down to that one little stone. It's the stone we should be obsessing about, not David. The stone gets us back to the power and promises of God. God put that giant down by supernaturally guiding that stone against all odds into his forehead so that He could redeem sinners. Sinners like Saul, David, and me. The point is not David, his character, or his courage. The point is the promise of God to do what He said He would do and the amazing way He accomplishes it.

Joseph and His Legendary Wardrobe

In a similar way, the story of Joseph is not the story of Joseph. It's not about his character or faith. It's the same story as David's but with a different time, place, and character. It too is about God's promise and the amazing way He brought a certain stage of it to pass. The point is not to emulate Joseph's life but to see how God did what He did through it.

Genesis 37:1-2 introduces us to Joseph's story and clearly states the purpose for his life.

Now Jacob lived in the land where his father had sojourned, in the land of Canaan. These are the records of the generations of Jacob.

Joseph, when seventeen years of age, was pasturing the flock with his brothers while he was still a youth, along with the sons of Bilhah and the sons of Zilpah, his father's wives. And Joseph brought back a bad report about them to their father.

You may ask, "Where do we find the purpose of Joseph's life in this passage?" It's right there in front of us. Remember Abraham, Isaac, and Jacob? "These are the records of the generations of Jacob." The reader is about to watch as the promises God made to Jacob and his descendants are preserved through some rather remarkable events involving Joseph. Later in the story as Joseph's father, Jacob, was dying, he set about blessing his sons. Here is what he said when he got to Joseph.

He blessed Joseph, and said,

"The God before whom my fathers Abraham and
   Isaac walked,
The God who has been my shepherd all my life to
   this day,
The angel who has redeemed me from all evil,
Bless the lads;
And may my name live on in them,
And the names of my fathers Abraham and Isaac;
And may they grow into a multitude in the midst
   of the earth" (Genesis 48:15-16).

You see it now? Abraham, Isaac, and Jacob. These are the patriarchs through whom the Messiah would come. The line of descendants comes right through Jacob and the life of Joseph. Genesis 37–50 is the account of God sustaining the promises to Jacob through Joseph. It is not about Joseph. Joseph could have been Bill.

The Real Story of Joseph

Here's the real story. A famine is on the way, a natural disaster that could completely destroy God's people. But God has made promises He must keep. Of course, the famine is ultimately something God Himself determined. So we know there are bigger things afoot than food supplies. God will use Joseph to protect this small people from devastation.

What happens blows my mind. God takes a ragtag group of people and elevates one of its members to the second-highest position of authority on earth. Obviously, things like this don't just happen. This certainly didn't happen because Joseph was an exceptionally gifted and capable person. After all, Joseph's wisdom and unique ability to interpret dreams were from God. They weren't natural gifts. What's more, these gifts were useless unless Joseph happened to be in the dank recesses of a Middle Eastern prison at the very moment he crossed paths with someone who spent more time near the ear of Pharaoh than anyone else.

That's exactly what happens. One day, when Pharaoh is struggling with dreams keeping him up at night, the cupbearer just happens to remember Joseph. Turns out fat and skinny cows are rather important. Who knew? Well, Joseph did. Everyone is saved. The rest is biblical history.

And once again, God did what He said He would do. But much more is here than meets the contemporary eye. As amazing as the preservation of a nation is, it's a subplot in the central story. God had sworn to multiply His people to a number beyond imagination. Remember the stars and Abraham? His family would grow from a meager tribe into a mighty nation rivaling the nations of the earth. This is exactly what he told Jacob.

> God appeared to Jacob again when he came from Paddan-aram, and He blessed him. God said to him,
>
> "Your name is Jacob;
> You shall no longer be called Jacob,

> But Israel shall be your name."
> Thus he called him Israel. God also said to him,
> "I am God Almighty;
> Be fruitful and multiply;
> A nation and a company of nations shall come
>   from you,
> And kings shall come forth from you.
> The land which I gave to Abraham and Isaac,
> I will give to you,
> And I will give the land to your descendants after
>   you" (Genesis 35:9-12).

But from where they stood at this moment—begging crumbs from the table of Egypt—that promise seemed impossible to fulfill. Enter Egypt. It's there for all to see if we will just look up. God had told Abraham exactly what would happen years before it came to pass.

> God said to Abram, "Know for certain that your descendants will be strangers in a land that is not theirs, where they will be enslaved and oppressed four hundred years. But I will also judge the nation whom they will serve, and afterward they will come out with many possessions" (Genesis 15:13-14).

How awesome is that! Israel did not run from a famine. They ran into the providential hand of God. They weren't captives at all. They were God's people on their way to becoming a great nation. In fact, they grew so rapidly, their population snuck up on the Egyptians. The Egyptians didn't know what to do with them. The opening lines of Exodus pick up the story as if it's the very next chapter in the same book. Of course, it is.

> The sons of Israel were fruitful and increased greatly, and multiplied, and became exceedingly mighty, so that the land was filled with them.

> Now a new king arose over Egypt, who did not know Joseph. He said to his people, "Behold, the people of the sons of Israel are more and mightier than we. Come, let

us deal wisely with them, or else they will multiply and
in the event of war, they will also join themselves to those
who hate us, and fight against us and depart from the land"
(Exodus 1:7-10).

It's so powerful when you realize that God put the testimony of
His faithfulness to His people in the mouth of a pagan Egyptian.
"Behold, the people of the sons of Israel are more and mightier than
we." Ironically, when the Egyptians tried to keep the Israelites from
departing, they actually initiated their departure. By leaning on the
Israelites they knocked over a series of dominoes God had set up
in ages past. You can see them fall one by one. Edicts. Baby Moses.
Wicker baskets. Riverbanks. Egyptian daughters. Adoption. A dead
Egyptian. A burning bush. Plagues. Gold rush. Water. Dry land.
Drowned Egyptians.

How amazing is our God? Who cares about Joseph? As important
as we think Joseph is, had he not faded from the Egyptians' mem-
ory, the real story would not have unfolded. "Now a new king arose
over Egypt, who did not know Joseph." I suppose the point is obvious. Someone greater than Joseph is necessary. A greater deliverance
is yet to come. This is the real story. One greater than Abraham, Isaac,
Jacob, Joseph, and Moses is on the way. Hear it rumble.

It's funny, really, when you think about it. The Egyptians think
they own the Israelites as slaves. Turns out, God was holding the
Egyptians captive by the presence of the Israelites. After all, this is the
only captivity Israel suffered that did not result from their disobedience. Once His purposes with Egypt were done, His people walked
out through water on dry land.

If we focus too closely on the character of Joseph and the specific
details of his internal struggles (which we don't know much about),
we miss the point of Joseph's life altogether. There is more here. Certainly, more than Joseph. In reality, the main character is God. God
is the subject. Not Joseph. In the end, the events surrounding Joseph's
life in Genesis were necessary because Joseph was a sinner in need of a
Savior. Joseph knew it was not about him. We often quote but rarely
understand his famous summary of his life.

> Joseph said to them, "Do not be afraid, for am I in God's
> place? As for you, you meant evil against me, but God
> meant it for good in order to bring about this present result,
> to preserve many people alive" (Genesis 50:19-20).

In other words, "What happened to me was not primarily about me. It was about God's faithfulness to a helpless people. What He did to me was for His glory and His name."

Now you can see why the things that happened to Joseph were necessary for something bigger than Joseph. It was necessary that the brothers despise their younger brother's privileged position as manager of the family business. Their angst had nothing to do with his superior character. The "coat of many colors" was necessary so his brothers could see him coming from far away and have enough time to plan an assassination. The coat, which his father gave him as a sign of love, was the very thing that doomed Joseph. Reuben's change of heart was necessary because Joseph must be kept alive, not because Reuben had a conscience. Down in a well Joseph goes. Perfect murder, right? Think again. It was necessary that an Ishmaelite slave caravan should come through at this very moment. After all, this was Joseph's transport to Egypt.

> Then they sat down to eat a meal. And as they raised their
> eyes and looked, behold, a caravan of Ishmaelites was com-
> ing from Gilead, with their camels bearing aromatic gum
> and balm and myrrh, on their way to bring them down
> to Egypt. Judah said to his brothers, "What profit is it for
> us to kill our brother and cover up his blood? Come and
> let us sell him to the Ishmaelites and not lay our hands on
> him; for he is our brother, our own flesh." And his broth-
> ers listened to him. Then some Midianite traders passed
> by, so they pulled him up and lifted Joseph out of the pit,
> and sold him to the Ishmaelites for twenty shekels of silver.
> Thus they brought Joseph into Egypt (Genesis 37:25-28).

Then Moses subtly inserts this statement into the narrative: "Meanwhile, the Midianites sold him in Egypt to Potiphar, Pharaoh's officer, the captain of the bodyguard" (verse 36).

"Meanwhile"? Are you kidding me? You can't make this stuff up. Our God is so great. I'm riveted. The psalmist understood the point of the story.

> Sing for joy to God our strength;
> Shout joyfully to the God of Jacob.
> Raise a song, strike the timbrel,
> The sweet sounding lyre with the harp.
> Blow the trumpet at the new moon,
> At the full moon, on our feast day.
> For it is a statute for Israel,
> An ordinance of the God of Jacob.
> He established it for a testimony in Joseph,
> When he went throughout the land of Egypt.
> I heard a language that I did not know:
> "I relieved his shoulder of the burden,
> His hands were freed from the basket.
> You called in trouble and I rescued you;
> I answered you in the hiding place of thunder;
> I proved you at the waters of Meribah." Selah
>   (Psalm 81:1-7).

Much later in the story of Joseph, after all the cool stuff happens and right before he dies, he reminds his brothers of God's promise to the patriarchs.

> Joseph said to his brothers, "I am about to die, but God will
> surely take care of you and bring you up from this land to
> the land which He promised on oath to Abraham, to Isaac
> and to Jacob" (Genesis 50:24).

And so the promise rolls on. Such power puts me on my face before a God who went to such incredible lengths to deliver me from something greater than the hand of Pharaoh. I love this story. If Joseph does not put on that coat and walk into that field and go down in that well, mankind is doomed. Why would I want to read anything into this? It is so much greater than the story we tell. It is a magnificent unfolding.

The Brightness of a Thousand Lesser Lights

As it is, the magnificent unfolding of redemptive history is constantly driven from our view by countless lesser lights. Preachers and authors have left us to assume that we're the main characters in this story. As we tell it, the Bible, its events and figures, all meander back to us and the quality of our lives. Somehow principles, steps, handbooks, therapies, programs, and slogans that constantly work *us* into the story line push the transcendent realities to the margins of the real events. We dismiss God and Christ from the center of the story about as casually as we shoo a cat off a couch. Rather than staring into the greatness of God's redemption and asking, "How can such a great God know my name?" we're transfixed by lesser things (sex, marriage, children, money, happiness, and garages). We raise our faces to the sky and whine, "When will God get around to improving my life?" We forget that He knows our names, and we wonder if He knows our routing number.

We've been told countless times (directly and indirectly) that our life's purpose and personal happiness are the central plots of the Bible. The members of the Trinity are merely a supporting cast in the story of *us*. God is an extra, standing unsuspectingly in the background of the epoch of human happiness. This narcissistic approach to the Bible obstructs our view of the greater glory before us. It's like that tall guy who inevitably sits in front of you at the movie theater. You never quite see the entire screen. The only difference is that we're the ones blocking our own view. As city lights crowd out the magnitude of space in the night sky, the magnificent reality of what God is doing is washed from view by lots of *us*. There is a much greater story than *us*. Right there above us is an infinity that takes our breath. To really see it, we must dim *us*. The smaller we are, the better the Bible reads. Seriously. The scope of the Bible is beyond vast. It sizes up the individual human being in its first few words. "In the beginning…" is a breathtaking opening line. No other record of human history starts where the Bible starts because none can. You can sense its depth. It sizes us up.

There are a dozen spiritual-sounding one-liners floating around in Christian circles regarding the Bible and its relevance to us. We consider them to be signs of spiritual depth.

How does this apply to my life?
How will Sunday's sermon affect me on Monday?
Where are the principles that will change my life?
Where's the application to my marriage?
How can this make me a better wife?
What's the takeaway value of this lesson?

There's nothing spiritual or noble in these questions. They are telltale signs of the popular view of the Bible, but they are all the wrong questions. We ask, "How do the pages relate to my life?" We *should* be asking, "How does my life relate to what's happening in these pages?"

The Bible always relates to us because it encompasses the entirety of humanity. It's relevant to you because it contains you. You are in it, but you are not the subject of it. God is the subject. It unfolds. Promises lead to a coat of many colors. An unlikely king leads to a stone flying over the desert. Coats and stones lead to crosses. Crosses lead to me. It's all there. Go read it and watch the expanse of God's grace run over where you stand. Be humbled. Be small and enjoy the story of God's grace in Christ. You are somewhere in that. Stop looking for the moral in the story and start enjoying it.

6

Rereading It All Over Again

Why do we bind up this collection between the same two covers, call it The Holy Bible, and treat it as one book? One justification for doing this—one of many—is that the collection as a whole, once we start to explore it, proves to have an organic coherence that is simply stunning. Books written centuries apart seem to have been designed for the express purpose of supplementing and illuminating each other. There is throughout one leading character (God the Creator), one historical perspective (world redemption), one focal figure (Jesus of Nazareth, who is both Son of God and Savior), and one solid body of harmonious teaching about God and godliness. Truly the inner unity of the Bible is miraculous: a sign and a wonder, challenging the unbelief of our skeptical age.

J.I. PACKER

At this point there may be an elephant in the room. How we've been handling the Bible for years is wrong. There are many who may be of the opinion that I'm throwing the baby out with the bathwater. Morals drawn from the life of the saints are still important. Actually, I'm not throwing out the baby. Rather, I'm asking, which is the baby and which is the bathwater?

Regardless, for those of us who've been reading the Bible wrongly, a rather important question remains. How do we start over? What are we supposed to do with the Bible if it's not a spiritual handbook? Where do we begin?

You begin with Christ. That's where Christ Himself began. Remember the story of the disciples on the road to Emmaus? Remember what the stranger on the road said to them after they recounted the events of the passion to Him?

> "O foolish men and slow of heart to believe in all that the prophets have spoken! Was it not necessary for the Christ to suffer these things and to enter into His glory?" Then beginning with Moses and with all the prophets, He explained to them the things concerning Himself in all the Scriptures (Luke 24:25-27).

Can you imagine how paradigm-shifting this must have been? How fortunate were these two unsuspecting disciples? A free seminary course on Jesus by Jesus Himself. Jesus retelling the story of Jesus. Beginning with Moses, He made his way through the Old Testament and recovered the Bible from the contemporary translation circulating around first-century Judaism. What was He pointing out as He walked them through Genesis, Exodus, Leviticus, Numbers, and Deuteronomy? *Himself.* The grace of God in Christ. Jesus is the point. Once Jesus left them, they were devastated—but in a good way. "They said to one another, 'Were not our hearts burning within us while He was speaking to us on the road, while He was explaining the Scriptures to us?'" (verse 32).

Jesus likely began in Genesis with God's promise to crush the serpent and then proceeded to show them all the links from one promise, patriarch, person, event, covenant, miracle, message, Law, and captivity after another until He got to the empty tomb. "It's about Me." How startling. He completely recast their understanding of the Old Testament. They would have been trained in the Old Testament from childhood. How scary is it to know that you can be so close to the truth and never put it together, never see it? That's us.

More than once I've been standing in my closet looking for a specific shirt that I can't seem to find. I call down to my wife, "Honey, I can't find my shirt."

"I put it in your closet."

"It's not in here."

This goes back and forth for a minute or two until she leaves what she's doing and makes her way upstairs to the closet. She walks right up to the shirt hanging directly in front of me and picks it up. "I put it in your closet." I hate that.

Jesus did the same thing to these guys. He walked them into a different hemisphere and pointed out something they could not see from where they previously stood. He was right in front of them the entire time, blocked by tradition. They never saw it. He walked right up and pointed out what they had been missing. When He did, the Scriptures exploded with power. The pages came alive. They were no longer searching for a moral. They were learning about a person.

Jesus Himself constantly draws us back to the main point of the Bible. He points out what's right in front of us. According to Jesus, the story of the Bible is Jesus.

> The testimony which I have is greater than the testimony of John; for the works which the Father has given Me to accomplish—the very works that I do—testify about Me, that the Father has sent Me.
>
> And the Father who sent Me, He has testified of Me. You have neither heard His voice at any time nor seen His form. You do not have His word abiding in you, for you do not believe Him whom He sent.
>
> You search the Scriptures because you think that in them you have eternal life; it is these that testify about Me…
>
> Do not think that I will accuse you before the Father; the one who accuses you is Moses, in whom you have set your hope. For if you believed Moses, you would believe Me; for he wrote about Me. But if you do not believe his writings, how will you believe My words? (John 5:36-39,45-47).

Moses wrote of Jesus? How? Where? Trust me, He's there. What Jesus is saying is more remarkable than you might imagine. Moses composed the first five books of the Old Testament. We know this collection as the Pentateuch. Genesis, Exodus, Leviticus, Numbers, Deuteronomy. Moses's authorship is made clear in the Bible.

> These are the journeys of the sons of Israel, by which they came out from the land of Egypt by their armies, under the leadership of Moses and Aaron. Moses recorded their start- ing places according to their journeys by the command of the LORD, and these are their journeys according to their starting places (Numbers 33:1-2).

These first five books are primarily composed of history. They record a specific part of world history pertaining to Israel, stretching from the beginning of time until the moment Israel was constituted a nation and was prepared to enter the Promised Land. Through Israel, Jesus would come. According to Jesus, this very record of events con- tained in the Pentateuch is a record of Him. This is what He meant when He said, "If you believed Moses, you would believe Me; for he wrote about Me."

He did not mean that He was mysteriously hidden in the events or that you need an Orphan Annie decoder ring to find Him. You can't spiritualize the events and expect Jesus to magically appear. Obviously, typology and foreshadowing are part of the Old Testa- ment genre, but what He intended was bigger than these. He meant that Moses wrote down the story of Him. "When you read the theme of promise spanning the Bible, you are reading My story." All of these events and people in the Bible are (in one way or another) about how God the Father brought Christ to save sinners and recover His cre- ation from the consequence of our rebellion.

Grace on a Rampage

The whole of the Bible is an accounting of all that was involved in putting Jesus on the planet and saving the planet from the conse- quences of us. All of it. Beginning to end. That's what Jesus said— "It's about Me." The Bible is a constant accounting of the gospel of grace across the expanse of human history. A permanent record of the faithfulness of our God. We read it and rejoice. This is exactly how Israel was instructed to approach the Bible and read it.

The events Moses wrote down were intended to raise the hearts of God's redeemed over the clouds of their existence and set them on a greater glory. Psalm 105 is a perfect example of how this was done. It is a chronicle of God's faithfulness, one glorious event to the next.

> Oh give thanks to the LORD, call upon His name;
> Make known His deeds among the peoples.
> Sing to Him, sing praises to Him;
> Speak of all His wonders.
> Glory in His holy name;
> Let the heart of those who seek the LORD be glad.
> Seek the LORD and His strength;
> Seek His face continually.
> Remember His wonders which He has done,
> His marvels and the judgments uttered by His
>   mouth,
> O seed of Abraham, His servant,
> O sons of Jacob, His chosen ones!
> He is the LORD our God;
> His judgments are in all the earth.
> He has remembered His covenant forever,
> The word which He commanded to a thousand
>   generations,
> The covenant which He made with Abraham,
> And His oath to Isaac.
> Then He confirmed it to Jacob for a statute,
> To Israel as an everlasting covenant,
> Saying, "To you I will give the land of Canaan
> As the portion of your inheritance,"
> When they were only a few men in number,
> Very few, and strangers in it.
> And they wandered about from nation to nation,
> From one kingdom to another people.
> He permitted no man to oppress them,
> And He reproved kings for their sakes:

"Do not touch My anointed ones,
And do My prophets no harm" (verses 1-15).

Turning to the story of Joseph, the psalmist continues.

> And He called for a famine upon the land;
> He broke the whole staff of bread.
> He sent a man before them,
> Joseph, who was sold as a slave.
> They afflicted his feet with fetters,
> He himself was laid in irons;
> Until the time that his word came to pass,
> The word of the LORD tested him.
> The king sent and released him,
> The ruler of peoples, and set him free.
> He made him lord of his house
> And ruler over all his possessions,
> To imprison his princes at will,
> That he might teach his elders wisdom.
> Israel also came into Egypt;
> Thus Jacob sojourned in the land of Ham.
> And He caused His people to be very fruitful,
> And made them stronger than their adversaries
> (verses 16-24).

Picking up with Moses, the redemptive epic rushes on.

> He turned their heart to hate His people,
> To deal craftily with His servants.
> He sent Moses His servant,
> And Aaron, whom He had chosen.
> They performed His wondrous acts among them,
> And miracles in the land of Ham.
> He sent darkness and made it dark;
> And they did not rebel against His words.
> He turned their waters into blood
> And caused their fish to die.
> Their land swarmed with frogs

Even in the chambers of their kings.
He spoke, and there came a swarm of flies
And gnats in all their territory.
He gave them hail for rain,
And flaming fire in their land.
He struck down their vines also and their fig trees,
And shattered the trees of their territory.
He spoke, and locusts came,
And young locusts, even without number,
And ate up all vegetation in their land,
And ate up the fruit of their ground.
He also struck down all the firstborn in their land,
The first fruits of all their vigor.
Then He brought them out with silver and gold,
And among His tribes there was not one who
    stumbled.
Egypt was glad when they departed,
For the dread of them had fallen upon them
    (verses 25-38).

What's the point? "God is so faithful and merciful and mighty—His plans can never be thwarted." It's right there on every page. Go read it. Can you imagine how powerful this message was for the ancient reader? "God is doing what He said He would do!" The intended effect is the same for the modern reader. The Bible reveals over and over what was accomplished by the power of God. We're supposed to read it the same way the ancients did. The only difference is, we have the total story and all the details. The Old Testament saints only had a part of the story, a few details, and the hope of promise. The promise was the same, but the details were fewer.

All these died in faith, without receiving the promises, but having seen them and having welcomed them from a distance, and having confessed that they were strangers and exiles on the earth…

And all these, having gained approval through their faith,

did not receive what was promised, because God had provided something better for us, so that apart from us they
should not be made perfect (Hebrews 11:13, 39-40).

New Testament Christians are able to see the whole thing happen
from beginning to end on the pages of Scripture. The story rushes
forward from the earliest pages and picks up people and events along
the way until we arrive at a stable in Bethlehem, when a King greater
than David bursts on the scene. From here it rushes past us out of
the empty tomb to the end of the age. Jesus is the hero who overshadows all others.

He was faithful to Him who appointed Him, as Moses also
was in all His house. For He has been counted worthy of
more glory than Moses, by just so much as the builder of
the house has more honor than the house. For every house
is built by someone, but the builder of all things is God.
Now Moses was faithful in all His house as a servant, for a
testimony of those things which were to be spoken later;
but Christ was faithful as a Son over His house—whose
house we are, if we hold fast our confidence and the boast
of our hope firm until the end (Hebrews 3:2-6).

In the Gospels, the Promised One walks onto center stage as He
emerges from the covering of ancient mysteries. All those who have
read the story correctly immediately react upon meeting Him. When
Jesus was dedicated in the temple, Simeon, who had been living in
anticipation, rejoiced over the Lord's Christ. He knew the Bible was
about this One who would come.

Now Lord, You are releasing Your bond-servant to
    depart in peace,
According to Your word;
For my eyes have seen Your salvation,
Which You have prepared in the presence of all
    peoples,
A light of revelation to the Gentiles,
And the glory of Your people Israel (Luke 2:29-35).

John the Baptist knew the entire story was one of redemption, and it stretched back to the beginning of time. When Jesus approached the waters of baptism, John the Baptist made this declaration:

> The next day he saw Jesus coming to him and said, "Behold, the Lamb of God who takes away the sin of the world! This is He on behalf of whom I said, 'After me comes a Man who has a higher rank than I, for He existed before me'" (John 1:29-30).

The New Testament epistles are no different. They read the same way and are about the same event, although in more detail than any Old Testament saint ever imagined. The epistles go behind the scenes and give us a spectacular glimpse into the very heart of God. They are a detailed schematic of redemption. Is it any wonder the gospel-saturated book of Romans opens with the same redundant story as the Old Testament?

> Paul, a bond-servant of Christ Jesus, called as an apostle, set apart for the gospel of God, which He promised before-hand through His prophets in the holy Scriptures, concerning His Son, who was born of a descendant of David according to the flesh, who was declared the Son of God with power by the resurrection from the dead, according to the Spirit of holiness, Jesus Christ our Lord, through whom we have received grace and apostleship to bring about the obedience of faith among all the Gentiles for His name's sake, among whom you also are the called of Jesus Christ;
>
> to all who are beloved of God in Rome, called as saints: Grace to you and peace from God our Father and the Lord Jesus Christ (Romans 1:1-7).

It's the same incomprehensible story of God's sovereign grace from page to page. Same essential message. "Great Is Thy Faithfulness"! Our reply is no different from those who read parts of the same story centuries ago. "Look at all our God has done to save us by His mercy. How great is our God! He is so faithful to do what He promised!"

Considering the way we normally approach the Bible, is it any wonder we struggle to read it or enjoy it? We usually read the Bible desperately searching for spiritual enhancement or insight into our personal lives. We're looking for us. But it's not about us. It's about God working in Christ. No wonder consistent Bible reading is so challenging for so many Christians. When you fall into this amazing story, you can't help but be dragged into its pages. Obviously, the Bible does have spiritual benefit. It does help us understand who we are and the reality of our deeper struggles as human beings. This is made clear by the Bible itself.

> O how I love Your law!
> It is my meditation all the day.
> Your commandments make me wiser than my
>   enemies,
> For they are ever mine.
> I have more insight than all my teachers,
> For Your testimonies are my meditation.
> I understand more than the aged,
> Because I have observed Your precepts.
> I have restrained my feet from every evil way,
> That I may keep Your word.
> I have not turned aside from Your ordinances,
> For You Yourself have taught me.
> How sweet are Your words to my taste!
> Yes, sweeter than honey to my mouth!
> From Your precepts I get understanding;
> Therefore I hate every false way.
> Your word is a lamp to my feet
> And a light to my path (Psalm 119:97-105).

> All Scripture is inspired by God and profitable for teaching, for reproof, for correction, for training in righteousness; so that the man of God may be adequate, equipped for every good work (2 Timothy 3:16-17).

The word of God is living and active and sharper than any
two-edged sword, and piercing as far as the division of soul
and spirit, of both joints and marrow, and able to judge
the thoughts and intentions of the heart. And there is no
creature hidden from His sight, but all things are open
and laid bare to the eyes of Him with whom we have to do
(Hebrews 4:12-13).

Nonetheless, the overall subject of God's Word is Jesus Christ.
Ultimately, our exposure to God's grace in the cross of Christ found
on the pages of the Bible is what transforms us, changes us, and recovers our humanity.

The Most Climactic Anticlimactic
Story Ever Written

When I was in seminary, my wife and I lived in an apartment
complex populated by several couples attending our school. One evening as we were approaching our apartment, some dear friends stuck
their heads out their front door and invited us to watch a movie with
them. "We rented *Schindler's List*. We just started it. Come on over
and join us." I had a ton of schoolwork to get done for the following
day, so of course I took them up on their offer.

As we sat down, my friend, who was rewinding the VHS tape
(dating myself here), said, "So far, I don't get it. Not sure what all the
hype is about. The movie doesn't make much sense. The Jews were
released from the labor camps in the first ten minutes of the movie.
What could the rest of it be about?" It struck me as odd as well, so I
grabbed the tape case and looked at the label. It read, "*Schindler's List*,
part 2." He had put the ending of the movie in first. He had watched
the last part first. The rest was anticlimactic.

But in order to understand the Bible rightly, you have to view
the whole thing having seen the ending first. The ending makes the
beginning and everything in between make sense. The gospel is
the most continually climactic, anticlimactic ending of all time. It
never gets old. The more we understand that the promise made to

Abraham would ultimately be fulfilled in the life, death, and resurrection of Jesus Christ, the more extraordinary the events that transpired become. We can see it happening. The gospel makes the Old Testament come together. It was there all the way back in the promise made to Abraham. Back in the very beginning.

> Be sure that it is those who are of faith who are sons of Abraham. The Scripture, foreseeing that God would justify the Gentiles by faith, preached the gospel beforehand to Abraham, saying, "All the nations will be blessed in you." So then those who are of faith are blessed with Abraham, the believer (Galatians 3:7-9).

If you view the Bible as only a means to greater spirituality, you will struggle to read it. It won't make much sense at all. It will be random and fable-like. But if you understand the Old Testament to be the chronicle of the gospel event in history and the New Testament to be the explanation of it, culminating in the empty tomb and consummating at the end of all things, then you will read it. Your heart will be drawn to it. This is primarily because you will want to marvel at what God has done for you. You will be stunned by how each little event and grand outcome on the pages of Scripture was rushing toward the cross, where Christ accomplished salvation.

What a strange place we are in as Christians when we find ourselves having to be convinced or reminded that Jesus is the point of the Bible! It seems odd as a pastor to be in a position where I have to substantiate this premise among Christians. How far afield are we when we find ourselves resistant to the idea that the Bible is about the glory of God manifested in His unrelenting grace through the work of Christ?

 **Part 3**

The Church

Christians want to be a part of churches that are disruptive forces in the culture, not indistinguishable from it. These evangelical dissidents have no interest in overcorrecting and returning to the religion of their parents. The idea of forming fundamentalist conclaves and hiding at safe distances from the culture is unthinkable. They're not seeking asylum behind the walls of traditional church. What they want is the chance to throw grenades. They are hungry for the front lines.

Hanging On Until
Jesus Gets Back

*The church started as a missionary movement in
Jerusalem. It moved to Rome and became an institution.
It traveled to Europe and became a culture. It crossed
the Atlantic to America and became a big business.*

ROBERT WEBBER

*They were continually devoting themselves to the apostles'
teaching and to fellowship, to the breaking of bread
and to prayer. Everyone kept feeling a sense of awe; and
many wonders and signs were taking place through the
apostles. And all those who had believed were together, and
had all things in common; and they began selling their
property and possessions and were sharing them with
all, as anyone might have need. Day by day continuing
with one mind in the temple, and breaking bread from
house to house, they were taking their meals together with
gladness and sincerity of heart, praising God and having
favor with all the people. And the Lord was adding to
their number day by day those who were being saved.*

ACTS 2:42-47

Boredom Is a Very Underestimated Emotion

The American church is bored. You can feel it. The giant isn't sleeping so much as it's twiddling its thumbs. The frustration is palpable.

We've spent so much time asking, "What's my purpose as an individual?" we forgot to ask the greater question: "What's God's purpose for the church?" For all our emphasis on personal identity, we've no idea what our collective identity is. We've no real sense of what we're supposed to be doing as a people. The reality that defines all of us has been overshadowed by the likes of us.

Boredom creates a unique sort of desperation. As others have said, it's a very underestimated emotion. Evangelical Christians, especially young ones, are desperate to experience church as God intended. Younger Christians can feel pressed between the faith traditions of their parents and the shallow pragmatism of contemporary church models. The pendulum, as it always does, has swung. There is a desire to worship. D.A. Carson observed this reaction among young Christians.

> We start attending meetings because it is habit, or because it is the right thing to do, or because we know that the means of grace are important, but not out of a heart-hunger to be with God's people and to be fed from God's Word. Sermons are filled with clichés. There is little intensity in the confession, little joy in absolution, little delight in the gospel, little urgency in evangelism, little sense of privilege or gratitude in witness, little passion for the truth, little compassion for others, little humility in our evaluations, little love in our dealing with others. [1]

There is currently an intense push back against the failed strategy of marketing techniques and the narcissistic philosophy of seeker churches. The failure is now more than obvious. Designer religion for affluent Americans only works in the suburbs and is not designed to save. The trendy suburban seeker models have left a confused spiritual wasteland in their wake. The gospel is all but forgotten. The suburbs are the new burned-over district. Christians are leaving in droves, seeking more meaningful experiences of church. The church is suddenly getting off the couch and going outside.

Christians want to be a part of churches that are disruptive forces in the culture, not indistinguishable from it. These evangelical dissidents have no interest in overcorrecting and returning to the religion of their parents. The idea of forming fundamentalist conclaves and hiding at safe distances from the culture is unthinkable. They're not seeking asylum behind the walls of traditional church. What they want is the chance to throw grenades. They are hungry for the front lines.

I recognize this angst in my own church. My people are desperate to live somewhere between Acts 1 and Acts 28. We're collectively bemoaning the loss of the good old days, when the gospel was fresh, church services were spontaneous eruptions of worship, people lived sacrificially for each other, and the body of Christ was a force to be reckoned with. When churches rose up with such force, the community had no idea what hit it. Seriously, who wouldn't want this to be their experience of church? Shouldn't it be? Isn't the true gospel the same gospel? Aren't we the same sinners saved by grace? Aren't the lost the same lost? Isn't it the same Holy Spirit? Are we not the same church?

I realize the early church can get romanticized into oblivion. Naively, some imagine an early church with no struggles or complications. It's viewed through utopian lenses. Some Christians who have deep-seated resentment toward organized religion read their preferences into the context of the early church. Simple church and churches without walls are in vogue. They imagine a more organic church that utilizes structure and tradition without allowing either to rob the church of a sincerity of fellowship. I sympathize with this vision. It must be more than some idealized antiestablishment movement. Structure is necessary. Besides, to get an antiorganized church movement started, you have to organize yourself. Good luck mobilizing the gospel by unorganizing the church. The idea is more about making sure necessary things (organization, programs) don't marginalize the main thing.

> Many of our churches have become cluttered. So cluttered
> that people have a difficult time encountering the simple

and powerful message of Christ. So cluttered that many people are busy doing church instead of being the church.[2]

What I desire is a genuine sense of church, one that may include organization and tradition but that also transcends these things. The problem is never the structure but the people who eventually place their faith in it. What we're after—and what I pray for in our own congregation—is the ever-present awareness that we have been called out as individuals by the grace of God in our city. The common bond of His love in Christ has brought us together and made us a family of faith. Not an evangelical colony of spiritually minded separatists, but a gathering of the redeemed in Christ who have found each other and who gather to praise God around the substitutionary sacrifice of His only Son. I want believers to be awestruck, bumping into themselves as they come around corners of the mind-blowing realities of the gospel. I pray for churches that have a sense of living on the frontier even while being down the street from a SuperTarget.

Reread the Scripture passage at the beginning of this chapter. You don't get there by downsizing your personal world, practicing personal austerity measures, or adapting some romanticized model of church. Real church cannot be fabricated. You get there the same way the believers in Acts did—individual and corporate devastation over the grace of God. Luke called it "awe."

Taking Our Cues from Home Depot

Personally, I'm encouraged the seeker movement has run its course in the suburbs. Looking back, it's hard to see how we thought this approach to church was a good idea. I realize it comes from a good place. But when the strategy for finding a suitable location for a church plant is the same strategy Lowes and Home Depot use to determine store locations, we're officially off the reservation. The history books will not be kind to these past decades. Sadly, part of the responsibility of any pastor ministering in the suburbs is picking up the pieces of confusion the movement left behind. Seriously, what were we thinking? Did we really think that was church?

On nearly every level and at every turn we've designed church around the individual. Anymore, this is the assumed starting point. "What does Joe Suburb say he needs?" In so doing, we've radically altered the church of Christ. We've defanged the gospel. We should have been asking, "How do I most effectively give Joe Suburb what he actually needs?" The difference between the two approaches is vast. The former allows Joe to determine his needs and then shapes the gospel into a suitable solution. Joe is saved from what Joe wants to be saved from. The latter perspective is not searching for a relevant message at all. It already has it—the gospel of Jesus Christ. Salvation from the consequences of sin through the substitutionary death of Christ is what Joe really needs. Always.

This new generation of Christians has realized the irrelevance of our supposedly relevant messages. One glance at the rest of the world, and you instantly realize the inconsequence of our message. Honestly, do you think our messages have any relevance to the masses in the Sudan? Of course not. People get this. Clichés that once had a hypnotic effect on American Christians are nearly insulting. Bigger questions than "Who am I supposed to be?" are looming in people's hearts.

What is the Christian response to suffering?

How can we make a dent in the vast needs before us?

Should my greatest concern be the health of my portfolio?

What can I liquidate in order to do my part?

Do I really need so much house?

Should I leave my career and aim for the mission field?

Times have changed.

My sense is that Christians are frustrated by the irrelevance of the American church. We're somewhat embarrassed by our recent history and are now making up for lost time. You can see this being played out in the current focus on humanitarianism around the world. Hunger assistance, sanitation sciences, medical treatments, strategies of sustainability, microfinance, relief efforts, adoption…the list of global causes is growing.

Closer to home, this very same inclination has driven the urban church movement. Congregations are popping up in inner-city and low-income contexts. Not coincidentally, these locations are characterized by real needs and not felt ones. The impact of the church is immediate and real. As a result, church planting efforts in the inner city are underway on a massive scale. The new mission movement is away from the suburbs. Why this exodus? Christians are tired of playing church. They want to participate in something meaningful.

Regardless of your opinion of these trends, the migration is undeniable and currently underway. Christians want to break out of the self-focus of the past and join dynamic communities of faith. It's not hard to see where the yearning comes from. When you live among so much prosperity, it's tricky to maintain any sense of biblical church. The environment in which we live creates a gaping disconnect between our churches and the church that exploded onto the scene in Jerusalem. The various emphases of suburbianity rob the church of its primary identity and power. Under the popular model, we're not gathering to press our souls deeper into the mystery of grace in order to detonate our hearts in our culture with the love of God in Christ. Rather, we gather to focus on strategies for personal wholeness. Evangelism is left to specialists. Missions happens in distant lands. We hire the "goers" so we can stay close to home.

Think about what this does to our sense of things. Why does the average Christian from the suburbs become a raving evangelist while on a short-term mission trip but have a wavering commitment stateside? It's strange but true. The moment the plane lands in a third-world country, we go bananas for Jesus. We have to travel halfway around the world to experience the Christian life as it was meant to be. Why this disparity in our reactions?

Basically, the suburbs get in our heads. It's hard not to assume the best about people living in upper-middle-class neighborhoods. "Love your neighbor as yourself" means something different here. We moved out here partly to choose who our neighbor would be. In most other places, your neighbor is not a manageable feature of your existence.

It's nearly impossible to see our suburban context as a mission field. Mission fields are in underdeveloped countries. We don't hurt for affluent people as we drive by their massive homes. We hurt for those living in the unending huts and shanties of Africa. There you can feel the darkness. Here you can feel good about the future.

Mountaintop Moments in the Burbs

David Platt knows a thing or two about the dulling effects of the suburbs on the church. His bestselling book *Radical* is a direct result of his personal frustration with the phenomenon. Early in the book, Platt describes several scenes that led to the emphasis of his now worldwide ministry. Certain events triggered a landslide of questions in his own life. He describes them as he lays the groundwork for his "less is more" exhortation to American Christians. Most notable was the impact of stepping onto the multimillion-dollar facility at the Church at Brook Hills on his first Sunday as pastor. (Brook Hills is located in the heavily religious Southern city of Birmingham, Alabama. His context and mine are similar. I know exactly what he faces as a pastor.)

Platt had just returned from visiting the underground churches in Asia. The contrast between the two contexts was stark. In one place, the people risked everything in their devotion to Christ. Fellowship with the saints was a priceless treasure. Prayers were sincere. Bible teaching was like precious crumbs falling into the hearts of famished people. Nominal Christianity is a contradiction of terms where persecution exists.

Back on the other side of the world, his own church was a very different scene. In a word, it was comfortable. It was more like a carnival than a group of broken people. Literally, a church carnival was taking place the afternoon of his first Sunday. The lesson in Platt's mind? The church in the suburbs takes so much for granted.

In another instance, Platt was confronted with the disproportionate focus in his own denomination. Two stories were juxtaposed on the front page of a denominational publication. One celebrated the completion of a $23 million facility by one of its partnering churches. The other described a $5000 gift raised for the starving masses in the Sudan by all the partnering churches in the denomination. Twenty-three million dollars so that already apathetic American Christians could enjoy a comfortable church experience, and $5000 for people who were starving to death. For Platt, the contrast was intolerable. Something had gone very wrong in the suburban church.

Later in the same series of events, Platt was standing on a mountaintop in India overlooking a city dominated by the Hindu religion. It was a benchmark moment. As he looked out, his heart broke for the millions of people who had never heard the gospel. Countless individuals were lost in the confusion of their pagan religion. This moment jarred Platt's heart and ultimately put the pieces together for his life's calling. Eventually, Platt's vision for world missions burst on the scene with the publication of *Radical*. The book helped turn the heart of the American church toward those around the world who have tremendous financial needs. Incalculable good has resulted from that mountaintop moment. I'm eternally grateful he had the courage to write it down and confront us with it.

Yet despite all the positive results, a serious blind spot in our thinking about the gospel has been exposed. If we're convinced that materially rich suburbanites are less needy than those in third-world countries, we're missing the point of the gospel. They're not. Obviously, the humanitarian needs are much greater in India, but the spiritual needs exist in both places and to the same degree. Same sinners. Same gospel. Same holy God. Assuming that a more urgent need for the gospel exists in these "pagan" regions of the world than in a heavily churched and affluent America is a serious misunderstanding.

When we look out at the heavily churched and Christianized American suburbs, we should have the same reaction Platt did on that mountain in India. Our hearts should break. Countless people are lost in their religion. So much organized religion can only denote the presence of countless lost souls. We should weep for the numerous individuals who've been misled by the gospel-less message of self-help

HANGING ON UNTIL JESUS GETS BACK   183

that swept through the American landscape. Just like Platt in India, we have to assume the worst about those souls among those unending steeples if we are to have any meaningful impact as a church.

Here's what we have to get our heads around. The heavily churched American suburbs are among the greatest mission fields on earth. On some levels, the distinction we've made between reached and unreached people groups has kept us from seeing this. I understand why we speak in such terms and realize the strategic importance of demographics as it relates to effective mission efforts around the globe. But if we think the presence of so many churches and historic denominations constitutes effective evangelization, we're wrong.

Have you been to Europe lately? The Reformation and the modern world-mission movement began there. Despite this, right now it's one of the darkest spiritual places on the planet. It's heavily reached but in desperate need of being reached. In an eerily similar way, the American church landscape constitutes an unreached region of the world. The true gospel is sparse. We can't turn our backs on the suburbs. They need us to be the church once more.

Don't assume that the presence of so many churches constitutes an effective gospel witness. It doesn't. There is a colossal need here. For certain it's not like a third-world context, where humanitarian needs are overwhelming. I agree with Platt. American Christians need to get over their lust for comfort and get off their wallets. But part of the danger with the current emphasis is believing that humanitarianism is the core mission of Christianity. It isn't.

Humanitarianism is a means to gospel proclamation. The gospel is the goal and message of our faith. Don't misunderstand me. Humanitarianism is definitely part of our calling that much of the traditional church has neglected. Yet we must keep in mind that there is nothing uniquely Christian about humanitarianism. We did not come up with the concept. Plenty of secular organizations do a much better (and smarter) job than the evangelical church does. Simply because the humanitarian needs in the suburbs are less than other places in the world does not mean the people in minivans aren't in danger of perishing.

Missional Soccer Moms on the Front Lines

Trust me, if you live out here as a Christian, you're in the thick of an incredibly intensive spiritual battle. The suburbs wreak havoc on Christianity. You don't have to travel to a third-world country to be on the front line. It's on your doorstep. Some of us have to stay behind and dig in. After all, who is going to reach the guy with the bulky 401(k) and a membership to the private club? Answer: a believer with a similar portfolio and a membership to the same club. Who's going to reach the soccer mom waiting for practice to wrap up? Answer: the missional soccer mom with a kid on the same team.

Living as a Christian may be harder in the American suburbs than any other place in the world. My brothers in the Middle East, whom I've visited many times, have said this very thing to me. "I don't know how you remain faithful there. It's such a difficult place to live." Of course, as they say this to me we are within sight of craters left by suicide bombers. It means something coming from them. The challenge of remaining faithful where life is comfortable is no less difficult than remaining faithful where real hostility exists. In some ways it's more difficult.

Obviously, you will probably never be dragged out of your bed and tortured. But you will be lulled to sleep. For certain, we're not forced underground if we want to worship and celebrate the gospel. Our plight is different. We're forced to worship in a context where everyone assumes they know the gospel, where the gospel has been redefined, and where comfort is worshipped more than Christ. We're not threatened by persecution. We're threatened by assimilation. God warned His people about this very danger on numerous occasions.

> The LORD your God is bringing you into a good land, a land of brooks of water, of fountains and springs, flowing forth in valleys and hills; a land of wheat and barley, of vines and fig trees and pomegranates, a land of olive oil and honey; a land where you will eat food without scarcity, in which you will not lack anything; a land whose stones are

iron, and out of whose hills you can dig copper. When you have eaten and are satisfied, you shall bless the Lord your God for the good land which He has given you.

Beware that you do not forget the Lord your God by not keeping His commandments and His ordinances and His statutes which I am commanding you today; otherwise, when you have eaten and are satisfied, and have built good houses and lived in them, and when your herds and your flocks multiply, and your silver and gold multiply, and all that you have multiplies, then your heart will become proud and you will forget the Lord your God who brought you out from the land of Egypt, out of the house of slavery. He led you through the great and terrible wilderness, with its fiery serpents and scorpions and thirsty ground where there was no water; He brought water for you out of the rock of flint. In the wilderness He fed you manna which your fathers did not know, that He might humble you and that He might test you, to do good for you in the end. Otherwise, you may say in your heart, "My power and the strength of my hand made me this wealth" (Deuteronomy 8:7-17).

There is very little personal cost for being a believer in the States. Even that which we might call persecution is more akin to oversensitivity on our part. Fact is, we don't really know persecution. Nominalism thrives under these conditions. Seriously, there's little physical danger in being a committed Christian here. The real threat is apathy. Apathy is the more serious challenge believers face. It robs the church's fire of its oxygen.

I know your deeds, that you are neither cold nor hot; I wish that you were cold or hot. So because you are lukewarm, and neither hot nor cold, I will spit you out of My mouth. Because you say, "I am rich, and have become wealthy, and have need of nothing," and you do not know that you are wretched and miserable and poor and blind and naked, I advise you to buy from Me gold refined by fire so that you may become rich, and white garments so that you may clothe yourself, and that the shame of your nakedness will not be revealed; and eye salve to anoint your eyes so that you may see. Those whom I love, I reprove and discipline; therefore be zealous and repent (Revelation 3:15-19).

Remaining faithful to Christ may be more challenging when there is no price for doing so. It takes an awe-inspiring, spirit-endowed awareness of the gospel to live a radical life among so much prosperity and ease. Living in light of eternal things is difficult when material things are so abundant. We should not underestimate the war raging for our devotion and souls in the suburbs. Among many other things, Platt got this right. It is real.

But the final solution to the pervasive materialism in America is not asceticism or downsizing. Those are responses, not solutions. They are helpful, but they can't touch the heart issue behind materialism. The solution includes a redemptive vision that so transforms our perspective that we are able to live as if we owned nothing even while possessing everything we need. It includes a grace that allows us to possess without being possessed. The cross of Christ can compel you to live as if you were on the frontier of some unreached people group even as you live in the heart of capitalism.

The fact that people know the religious verbiage and routine makes our task even more challenging. Most people are inoculated to the word "gospel." Here you have to convince them they're lost before you can present them with the need to be saved. In India you naturally assume everyone is lost. In the American suburbs you can't assume people are saved even when they say they are.

Where I live, everyone thinks he's Christian. It's not like ministering the gospel in distant jungles or in more secularized regions of the United States. In these places individuals know they're not Christians, they don't want to be Christians, and they wish you would stop your appeals. But here, people consider you unkind if you dare question their spiritual condition. Evangelizing people who've been "saved" since birth takes raw gospel courage. The people we evangelize may not have bones in their noses or be bowing down to wooden idols. Indeed they are not. Their idolatry is much more sophisticated and entrenched than that. They've got killer Bible apps on their smartphones.

The true church in the suburbs is sitting on the edge of a massive revival. The malls are white for harvest. The true gospel is practically unknown out here. Everywhere you turn, a gospel conversation awaits. If you're looking to make an impact, the time is now. The message of the cross is an utterly disruptive force in these heavily religious areas. It always has been.

Ultimately, we're not that far removed from the conditions of the amazing gospel revolution that took place in the early days of the church. Same message. Same hardened sinners. Same Holy Spirit. Same Savior. We too can "upset the world," right here in the suburbs. I realize it's incredibly hard to have the same impassioned reaction to the masses living out here that we have to those in third-world countries, but we must. It is possible in the gospel. Even with that latte in your hand. It all depends on how you see it.

Jesus Was a Third-Rate Magician

I offer this modern parable.

Two men enter your church for the first time on the same Sunday morning. They could not be from more alternate universes. The first man is from where you are. Coat-and-tie territory. His sweet-faced wife and two well-dressed children are with him. They slightly resemble the family in the frame. By all accounts, they are decent people. They are quite possibly church hunting. After all, it is always open season in the suburbs. The presence of Bibles in hand may indicate they know the routine. They're churched. They mingle briefly at the end of the service and greet the pastor on the way out. You hope they come back.

The other man seems to be from nowhere. He's apparently homeless. All the signs are there. Matted hair, tattered clothes, filth, the stench of alcohol...in fact, the ragged little man is obviously intoxicated at this very moment. He lumbers in and sits in the back row without a word. He has that dispirited look that characterizes beggars. As you might expect, he stands out. You know that classic scene where the wrong type of person walks into a bar and the juke-box goes silent with a scratch of a record? Pin-drop silence. It's like that. But this is not a bar, it's church. The scene takes awkward to another level.

You can't help but notice him. Everyone notices him, including that other new guy with his family. In the back of your mind a cruel and unguarded thought escapes your well-adjusted conscious. "I hope the first guy doesn't think the homeless guy represents who we are as a church." The thought is quickly deleted. During the service you cannot take your eyes off this broken human being. Your heart breaks for him, as it should. Without casting judgment or assum-ing what landed him in his destitution, you decide to reach out to him after the service. The "other side of the tracks" is running right down the center of your church on this day. In the love of Christ you will step over them and the various lines of polite society that buffer you from such realities. How desperate he must be. How urgently he needs Jesus. You'll show this person the love of Christ. You make a beeline.

We'll leave the story there.

So, what's the lesson? You're probably thinking it's that our self-focus, comfort levels, biases, and jaded perception limit the extent of our compassion for other human beings. And you'd be right. We judge people based on appearances and superficial realities. We're selective about who we show the grace of God. We're blindly par-tial. People's conditions hold us back from loving them as we should. That's part of our problem. Isn't this the very prejudice at play in the above scenario? Of course it is. Our behavior toward this man is but an illustration of how we normally operate. What we do to this man solely because of the way he looks is shameful. Seriously, how can we treat the man in the suit so cruelly?

Wait—what? Not expecting that? Gotcha. It was that other bias I had in mind. The one that forces us to equate "spiritual" and "moral" with "Christian." It's this film over our eyes that keeps us from going bananas for Jesus in business parks.

The well-kept man is the real victim here. He's the one to whom no grace was shown. Why didn't you make a beeline for him? I'll tell you why. Because your bias and presupposition about the human condition that you picked up from the suburbs kept you from assuming the worst about the depth of his experience of the gospel. This same perspective allowed you to immediately assume the worst about the man in tatters.

Don't misunderstand me. You *should* assume the man in tatters hasn't experienced the transforming power of the gospel. That's not the issue. The issue is that you did not assume the same thing about both men. Hear me. You should assume the worst about *all* men's spiritual condition. If you're not as desperate for the guy in the suit as you are the guy in rags, your love is conditional.

If you're not also making a beeline for the man in the suit with the same type of broken heart, you misunderstand the gospel. If your heart doesn't sink with the man drowning in his affluence the way it did for the man drowning in alcohol, you don't get it. You're assuming he knows the gospel. You should be thinking the exact same thing you did about the bum.

"How desperately that guy in the suit needs Jesus. Look at him! He believes his morality and church attendance save him. Most likely, right now he's comparing himself to that homeless guy and assuming the best about his own condition. Oh, how blind he is! I've got to put the cross of Christ in his path. He needs to see himself as a leper and not a Republican."

This nearly imperceptible presupposition about human beings coats our souls in the suburbs, and it has robbed the church of its purpose and power. It's blurred our understanding about the human condition. According to our impulse, the really lost people are lying in urban alleys or searching for water in third-world contexts. Candidates for evangelism don't wear Brooks Brothers suits. Fact is, we struggle to evangelize the coats and ties because we never think to do it. They have such well-adjusted lives, there's nothing to deliver them from. This is why our message sounds like a free upgrade and not a free gift of redemption.

Question: Why do you suppose we don't walk through our malls with the urgency we have when we walk down our alleyways? In the malls, we're oblivious to people because everyone blends in to the general prosperity. In the alleyways we're horrified because everyone stands out as shattered. No one goes to malls when they are out of resources. No one living in an alley needs the malls. Malls don't give away free meals. In our minds, one need is more acute than the other.

We don't feel sorry for the guy driving the Beamer. We either envy or begrudge him. He has no needs. Humanitarianism has no place in his context. But we can't help but pity the guy living in his brand-new cardboard box. This is such a distorted vision. Is there such a great difference between these men before God? No. God judges them impartially.

> All of you who were baptized into Christ have clothed yourselves with Christ. There is neither Jew nor Greek, there is neither slave nor free man, there is neither male nor female; for you are all one in Christ Jesus. And if you belong to Christ, then you are Abraham's descendants, heirs according to promise (Galatians 3:27-29).

When it comes to the righteous standard of the Law, God gives no consideration to Beamers or boxes. We must keep in mind that each of these men is trapped in the same horrible condition. Driving new Beamers, of course.

Gotcha again. Man, this is easy.

> If you address as Father the One who impartially judges according to each one's work, conduct yourselves in fear during the time of your stay on earth; knowing that you were not redeemed with perishable things like silver or gold from your futile way of life inherited from your forefathers,

but with precious blood, as of a lamb unblemished and spotless, the blood of Christ (1 Peter 1:17-19).

Jesus spent an extraordinary amount of energy flipping this very perception in His own culture. Whether through explicit declarations or visuals, He was always turning the world upside down. Jesus invented the grenade Paul loved to throw.

> Do you not understand that everything that goes into the mouth passes into the stomach, and is eliminated? But the things that proceed out of the mouth come from the heart, and those defile the man. For out of the heart come evil thoughts, murders, adulteries, fornications, thefts, false witness, slanders. These are the things which defile the man; but to eat with unwashed hands does not defile the man (Matthew 15:17-20).

You know that magician's trick with the tablecloth? An eight-piece table setting complete with candlesticks stays put while the tablecloth is snatched from underneath. Yeah, that was Jesus on this point. Everywhere He went He announced, "Hey, watch this!" But every time He did, every delicate little cultural bias came crashing down. When Jesus was done, nothing was left but an empty table and shattered traditions. He was a terrible magician. Turns out He isn't a magician at all. He's a wrecking ball.

Jesus told the original version of my parable of the man in the suit. I totally ripped that off. We know it as the parable of the tax collector and the Pharisee.

> Two men went up into the temple to pray, one a Pharisee and the other a tax collector. The Pharisee stood and was praying this to himself: "God, I thank You that I am not like other people: swindlers, unjust, adulterers, or even like this tax collector. I fast twice a week; I pay tithes of all that I get." But the tax collector, standing some distance away, was even unwilling to lift up his eyes to heaven, but was beating his breast, saying, "God, be merciful to me, the sinner!" I tell you, this man went to his house justified

rather than the other; for everyone who exalts himself will be humbled, but he who humbles himself will be exalted (Luke 18:10-14).

The point is not to pity the one man and resent the other. We do that already. The point is that the two men, who represent poles in our perspective, need the same thing—the mercy of God and a righteousness outside their reach. Obviously, the Pharisee's perspective of the tax collector was self-righteous and judgmental. It was full of assumptions. What we seem to overlook is that the Pharisee's opinion of the tax collector was dead-on. The tax collector was a wicked sinner. The tax collector himself agrees with the Pharisee's assessment. Why else would he be there?

Additionally, the Pharisee wasn't wrong about all the stuff he did in the name of God. Indeed, he was zealous. The real issue is that the Pharisee thought those things saved him. But he couldn't see that he needed to repent of these good deeds instead of recounting them. Repenting in the same manner as the tax collector was the furthest thing from his mind. Everyone feels good about himself standing this close to a disaster. Nonetheless, one of these men is not more worthy than the other. One of these men is not more needy of grace. They are the same men. They only live on opposite sides of the tracks. One's dressed in a suit and one's dressed like a pimp, but they are the same man. It's just so hard to see it.

This blindness underlies Jesus's encounter with the rich young ruler. It's a critical event in the life of Christ and the disciples. A benchmark moment in the New Testament. The Gospels pay very close attention to it.

> Someone came to Him and said, "Teacher, what good thing shall I do that I may obtain eternal life?" And He said to him, "Why are you asking Me about what is good? There is only One who is good; but if you wish to enter into life, keep the commandments." Then he said to Him, "Which ones?" And Jesus said, "You shall not commit murder; you

shall not commit adultery; you shall not steal; you shall not bear false witness; honor your father and mother; and you shall love your neighbor as yourself." The young man said to Him, "All these things I have kept; what am I still lacking?" Jesus said to him, "If you wish to be complete, go and sell your possessions and give to the poor, and you will have treasure in heaven; and come, follow Me." But when the young man heard this statement, he went away grieving; for he was one who owned much property (Matthew 19:16-22).

The math in Jesus's day went something like this: Good + wealthy = blessed by God. In this man's case it was exponentially greater: Flawless + lavishly wealthy = God's prized pupil. Given the reaction of the onlookers (they are the ones you should pay attention to in the story), this man was a shoo-in for the kingdom. If good = godly and prosperous = saved, this guy is the Michael Jordan of religion. You want him on your team. But as you might expect, Jesus does the unexpected. Having the first pick in the religious draft, Jesus trades down to pick up the first person who will admit his failure and need for Him.

As Moses lifted up the serpent in the wilderness, even so must the Son of Man be lifted up; so that whoever believes will in Him have eternal life.

For God so loved the world, that He gave His only begotten Son, that whoever believes in Him shall not perish, but have eternal life (John 3:14-16).

Notice how Jesus immediately begins pulling the thread on His culture's concept of good? "Why are you asking Me about what is good? There is only One who is good."

That's not even where the young man was going, but it's where Jesus takes him. Why? Because "good" was his real problem. He was estimating himself and other people based on the math of self-righteousness. "There is only One who is good" is the exact moment

Jesus snatched the assumption off the table. When Jesus pressed him to examine himself in light of the Law, the young man should have fallen to his knees. Instead he stood toe-to-toe with God. "All these things I have kept, what am I still lacking?"

That's insanity, but religious people do it all the time. They try to stare down a holy God with filthy rags. Now you know why Jesus went around preaching the Sermon on the Mount. "You have heard it said...but I say to you..." It's not the letter of the Law, but the heart of the Law that matters before God. The rich young man was blind to his own sin because he suffered from the same biases we do. I'd guess this was the first time this man had ever been evangelized. There goes Jesus, contradicting everything we believe again. He made a beeline for the good guy.

Worlds collide here. If this man's assumption about himself is true, then the truth about Jesus is not. Why in the world is Jesus on earth? What's Jesus here for if not to offer His life for this man's? Even highly respected men need a substitute. Jesus's very presence is an implication about every man. The incarnation is the smudge on our good opinions of ourselves.

When we get to the part where Jesus tells the man to sell his possessions and follow Him, we usually misunderstand the exchange or read it through our contemporary lens. Jesus wasn't calling this man to a life of asceticism. That was not Jesus's gospel. Spiritual austerity and godliness are not mutually inclusive. To take Jesus's confrontation this way is to espouse a gospel of works. No one is saved by works. This man would not have been saved through a yard sale.

The issue is not his wealth. It's what he thought his wealth represented. Jesus was getting down to his real need. Despite (or because of) the ornate condition of his life, he did not see himself as a spiritual leper. He didn't need Jesus. He wanted Jesus to acknowledge the quality of his life and assume that his spiritual destination was secure. But the Lord drops some unheard-of math. Good + wealthy = lost. It's like saying one + one = zero. Jesus doesn't assume anything about the man's spiritual condition.

> Jesus said to His disciples, "Truly I say to you, it is hard for a rich man to enter the kingdom of heaven. Again I say to you, it is easier for a camel to go through the eye of a needle, than for a rich man to enter the kingdom of God." When the disciples heard this, they were very astonished and said, "Then who can be saved?" And looking at them Jesus said to them, "With men this is impossible, but with God all things are possible" (Matthew 16:23-26).

"Who can be saved?" This may be the first appropriate question the disciples asked. They couldn't believe what they heard, but they heard it right. Without realizing it, they got it. The effect of this exchange was like shrapnel. Essentially, their question gets right down to it. "If he's not in, who is?" All assumptions are blown to bits at this very moment. No one who thinks he is outside of a need for Jesus gets in. Everyone who acknowledges his need for Jesus does. Grace through faith alone. Good people need to repent.

It's possible to misunderstand the point of this exchange from a different direction. Jesus's point is not to say poor people are easier to save than wealthy people. It's just as impossible for people living in boxes to be saved. To assume otherwise is also a denial of the gospel. Basically, it is impossible for *any* man to save himself through works. The rich young man represented the pinnacle of works righteousness. If he can't save himself, who has any hope?

Jesus reinforced their dilemma by using the image of the eye of a needle. They needed to feel the conflict. "Despite what you have been led to believe, this man is not going to heaven. He needs Me the same way you need Me." There is no discernible difference between people before God. All have sinned. Making a beeline for the rich young ruler requires a paradigm shift only the gospel can effect.

Until you feel the urgent need to expose the guy with the fat bank account to the real tragedy in his life, you're missing the point of Jesus. Until you realize that the greatest need of the guy in the alley is not a meal, you're missing the emphasis of the gospel. When we flee the suburbs to plant urban churches because we assume lower-income contexts will be more susceptible to the gospel, we're naive. In fact, we're beyond self-righteous. And when we stomp away from the heavily churched suburbs, assuming the people there get enough exposure to the gospel, we're no less naive. As we have seen, the vast majority have not been exposed to the gospel.

The Church as Strategy

*Here, surely, is the most challenging
missionary frontier of our time.*

LESLIE NEWBIGIN

*You are a chosen race, a royal priesthood, a holy nation,
a people for God's own possession, so that you may
proclaim the excellencies of Him who has called you out
of darkness into His marvelous light; for you once were
not a people, but now you are the people of God; you had
not received mercy, but now you have received mercy.*

1 PETER 2:9-10

"Do you have an evangelistic program?"

I've been asked this question countless times by newcomers over the years. It's a legitimate question. The answer has varied. It all depends on when I was asked. Sometimes it was a definitive yes. Other times it was an awkward no. At times there were classes on evangelism underway. Other times there weren't. Always, it was assumed we were talking about a sequenced and formatted evangelistic training class. Sessions followed by outings. Cars, maps, addresses, and flashlights. Visitors beware. In other words, specialization. Whether they intended it or not, what I heard them ask was, "Do you care about lost people?" Obviously, it was very painful when the answer happened to be no. The implications of no run deep.

Like every other church, ours has tried various angles to spark a spirit of evangelism in our congregation. After all, we should be

evangelizing. The Bible is clear on this. Over the years we've imple-
mented all kinds of approaches in an effort to get the fire started. I so
badly wanted to answer yes.

We've done a little bit of everything. Evangelistic training sessions
that included outings with experienced evangelists as mentors. Cold
calls to neighbors around us. Inner-city outreaches. Campus outreaches. Special-event outreaches. Seasonal outreaches. Humanitarian outreaches. Rescue-mission outreaches. Distributions of tracts at
malls and large public places. Public preaching. We paid house calls to
visitors. We put pins on maps. We developed surveys. We did and
still do a lot of these things. They all met with some success. They
touched the lives of people who participated, and by God's grace,
some people were saved.

But some basic problems existed no matter what we did. For one,
the majority of these programs or approaches never endured. Volun-
teers disappeared and momentum faded. Even if they did endure, the
same frustrated folk rotated through them. We were always coming
back to square one, looking for a new angle to mobilize the church.
Furthermore, and maybe more importantly, many of these efforts
resulted in canned approaches. People were memorizing and reciting
things that seemed to be useful for one context but not another.
Working off a script can be helpful, but remembering it can be
challenging. Ultimately, our methods did not seem to translate into
real life. "We evangelize on Wednesday evenings" was just as dissatis-
fying an answer as no. I came to one basic conclusion. We may have
been evangelizing, but we were not necessarily becoming evangelistic.
There's a huge difference.

I began to ask some questions. Is this approach to evangelism right?
Should we aim for programs, methods, and approaches like these? Is
this what God wants us to be doing? I searched out an answer. I went
back to square one. I read the Bible in an attempt to find a specific
method of evangelism. What I came to understand was striking.
The very question, "Does your church have an evangelistic program?"
is loaded with misunderstanding. The more I studied, the more I

realized that introducing techniques for the sake of evangelism could actually be counterproductive to evangelism.

I wanted evangelism to be the rule and not the exception. In some ways I was working against the very thing I prayed God would accomplish. If I wanted to create an evangelistic heart in our church and myself, I would have to radically alter my thinking. Not about evangelism and missions per se but about the church itself. Going back to the Word, reading the Gospels, the book of Acts, and the Epistles, challenged all my presuppositions. I observed something completely different from what I had known. To my surprise I actually found an evangelistic program. One that is always on tap. One that works in amazing ways. One that creates a spirit of evangelism. One that makes evangelism the rule and not the exception.

God's program for evangelism is the local church. Sinners redeemed within and from every layer of a community who gather and scatter in the same community. Novel idea, I know, but it's true. The Bible assumes that the church exists to proclaim the gospel from the platform of redeemed lives. God's program for the evangelization of the world is you. It's the redeemed, swelling the ranks of local churches with hearts full of grace and truth, spilling out into the communities where they may live.

All the little techniques might enhance this effort, but they are secondary at best. What creates an evangelistic heart in the church are individual broken ones. The devices we use are simply means. The end is the glory of God through the proclamation of the gospel and the salvation of sinners—proclamation to sinners by sinners. The church is not free group therapy or a spiritual social club. We are the church. God ordained the local church for the very purpose of spreading the message of His grace to the glory of His name.

What's most critical to missions is not so much how we understand missions, but how we view the church. In the Bible, the church and missions are interchangeable realities. The separation we've created with our modern concept of world missions is somewhat of a misnomer. The church is God's strategy for the evangelization of the world.

If we view church primarily as people who gather weekly to enhance our lives through a download of biblical-sounding spiritual information, a missional temperament will always be challenging. Evangelism will be an afterthought. Missions will be a line item on our budget and not a part of a heartbeat. On the other hand, if the church views itself as a mission effort planted on the frontier of its community, missions will be integral. As it turns out, this is exactly who we are.

> But you are a chosen race, a royal priesthood, a holy nation, a people for God's own possession, so that you may proclaim the excellencies of Him who has called you out of darkness into His marvelous light; for you once were not a people, but now you are the people of God; you had not received mercy, but now you have received mercy (1 Peter 2:9-10).

We were chosen by a gracious God not only to enjoy the benefits of His grace but also to extend those benefits to sinners through our lives and the proclamation of the gospel. We are worshippers and grace proclaimers. We gather on Sundays not to avoid the world, but to prepare to invade it on Mondays. According to Scripture, church starts on Monday, not Sunday morning.

> You are the salt of the earth; but if the salt has become tasteless, how can it be made salty again? It is no longer good for anything, except to be thrown out and trampled under foot by men.

> You are the light of the world. A city set on a hill cannot be hidden. Nor does anyone light a lamp and put it under a basket, but on the lampstand, and it gives light to all who are in the house. Let your light shine before men in such a way that they may see your good works, and glorify your Father who is in heaven (Matthew 5:13-16).

Church is not a place we go. Church is who we are. It may gather in a specific location, but come Monday it scatters to a thousand nooks and crannies in the community. If we can get here in our understanding, evangelism will be the rule and not the exception. The idea of extending the gospel into our communities will be an ordinary part of our conversations and not an exceptional one.

As it is, we've adopted a view of church that parallels American domestic objectives more than it does biblical ones. It conflicts directly with the mission of Christ. "For even the Son of Man did not come to be served, but to serve, and to give His life a ransom for many" (Mark 10:45).

The perspective of the suburban church is a major deterrent to our sense of missions. Our lives are primarily about making it to retirement. Out there somewhere a plateau of existence is waiting for us. Once we find it, we coast into the eternal state. Between here and there, we just try to maintain our contentment and spirituality. These life goals have tainted our eternal ones. The church is more or less a group of very busy part-time spiritualists. We're just attempting to hang on until Jesus gets back. We're white-knuckling our way to glory. We're isolationists, hunkering down in our ecclesiastical bunkers, waiting for the trumpet blast.

In and Not of but Definitely In

You know that biblical saying that we so often hear? "In the world but not of the world"? We use this to reinforce our separatist ecclesiology. It's like a slogan written above the front doors in our homes, reminding us to keep ourselves out of the path of the world. Stay off the streets at night. Pull your shades on Halloween and kill the lights. This is because we emphasize the "not of" aspect and ignore the rest. What about the "in"? We miss the actual point of the expression. Are we not in the world while not being of it? Allow me to restate this mantra with a more biblical emphasis. "In and not of but definitely in!"

> The eleven disciples proceeded to Galilee, to the mountain which Jesus had designated. When they saw Him, they worshiped Him; but some were doubtful. And Jesus came

up and spoke to them, saying, "All authority has been given
to Me in heaven and on earth. Go therefore and make disciples of all the nations, baptizing them in the name of the
Father and the Son and the Holy Spirit, teaching them to
observe all that I commanded you; and lo, I am with you
always, even to the end of the age" (Matthew 28:16-20).

For many of us, our view of the church prioritizes avoiding the
influence of the secular culture until Jesus rescues us. We practice
an "evade and escape" ecclesiology. We're not evangelists as much
as we are doomsday preppers. Our tactics are isolation, separation,
and avoidance. Church is where the moral people who had the good
sense to become Christians hide for spiritual survival. In the suburbs
we have our own brand of secret church. Somehow, in the strangest twist, the unsaved are our enemy. Those whose ideologies oppose
traditionally conservative ideologies—LGBTs, social liberals, and so
on—are all the mortal enemies of the church. Ultimately, they pose
no greater threat to a consistent gospel witness than conservatives do
when social conservatism is confused in biblical Christianity. Ironically, the church seems angry at the lost in our culture for being lost.
"Go" has come to mean "Get away from." What this exposes about
our understanding of the gospel is tragic.

Not long ago I was invited to a Christian seminar on restoring
a biblical worldview in America. Apparently, America was once a
Christian nation populated by born-again believers. Somehow I
missed this little detail while earning my history degree in college.
No doubt what the seminar was really about was the restoration of
a Judeo-Christian ethic and morality in the United States. It was all
about curbing the rising tide of nontraditional values in America.

Obviously, America is founded on a principle of religious freedom and is governed—for the most part—by a Judeo-Christian ethic.
Furthermore, there is little doubt that these foundational principles
have begun to erode in our culture. We are more and more a secular nation. But we fail to realize that Christian ethics and morality
are not the same as a Christian worldview. Only those who are born

again operate with a Christian worldview. A Christian worldview is utter foolishness to the world—even to the world of the moral and religious.

> The word of the cross is foolishness to those who are perishing, but to us who are being saved it is the power of God. For it is written,
>
> "I will destroy the wisdom of the wise,
> And the cleverness of the clever I will set aside."
>
> Where is the wise man? Where is the scribe? Where is the debater of this age? Has not God made foolish the wisdom of the world? For since in the wisdom of God the world through its wisdom did not come to know God, God was well-pleased through the foolishness of the message preached to save those who believe. For indeed Jews ask for signs and Greeks search for wisdom; but we preach Christ crucified, to Jews a stumbling block, and to Gentiles foolishness, but to those who are the called, both Jews and Greeks, Christ the power of God and the wisdom of God (1 Corinthians 1:18-24).

Restoring a "biblical worldview" to American culture and politics will not save a single soul. This is not the mission of the church. Only the gospel saves, and only on an individual basis. Any discussion about restoring America to its Christian roots that focuses on the legislation of morality rather than the proclamation of the gospel is off from the start.

Among the hot-button topics to be discussed at this seminar was abortion. How can the various pro-life outlets in America work together to challenge the ongoing genocide of the most helpless among us? The statistics are startling. In 2008, according to the Centers for Disease Control, there were 1.2 million legal abortions in the United States of America. In 2008 in New York City there were 732 abortions for every 1000 live births. By far, the majority of abortions occur due to matters of convenience. Three-quarters of those who had abortions in 2008 did so because having a baby interfered with a standard of living. Since 1973 there have been 50 million abortions in this country. For certain, the sanctity of life is of little concern for many Americans. The right to choose applies to everyone except those who have no choice at all.

Abortion is a great and unthinkable evil. One of the greatest indictments against our nation to date. It's hard not to get emotional while discussing it in either religious or political arenas. As a believer, it's impossible to have any other position than pro-life. The sanctity of life is in the DNA of our faith. "You shall not murder." Naturally, the church should be a part of the efforts to stop abortion in this country. Sanctity of life is a vital part of a Christian worldview. We cannot sit idly by and let innocent lives be slaughtered without protesting—and still consider ourselves Christian.

And the Christian worldview takes us much further than this. It demands not only that we defend the innocent but also that we love the guilty. This is where a truly Christian outlook transcends Judeo-Christian ethics. We know we are viewing life from a truly Christian perspective when we are as desperate for those who choose to take an innocent life as we are for those whose lives were taken.

> But I say to you who hear, love your enemies, do good to those who hate you, bless those who curse you, pray for those who mistreat you. Whoever hits you on the cheek, offer him the other also; and whoever takes away your coat, do not withhold your shirt from him either. Give to everyone who asks of you, and whoever takes away what is yours, do not demand it back. Treat others the same way you want them to treat you. If you love those who love you, what credit is that to you? For even sinners love those who love them. If you do good to those who do good to you, what credit is that to you? For even sinners do the same. If you lend to those from whom you expect to receive, what credit is that to you? Even sinners lend to sinners in order to receive back the same amount. But love your enemies, and do good, and lend, expecting nothing in return; and

your reward will be great, and you will be sons of the Most
High; for He Himself is kind to ungrateful and evil men.
Be merciful, just as your Father is merciful (Luke 6:27-36).

An Alternate Christian Universe

Our separationist strategies have created a very bizarre Christian
subculture. We're not *in* at all. We're completely *out*. We're almost
entirely absent. This emphasis touches everything—science, art, politics, education. Rather than having Christians who enter into politics,
we have Christian politicians. The result is the legislation of morality
and not gospel proclamation among world influencers. Rather than
Christians who happen to be artists, we have Christian artists. The
results include very cheesy third-rate movies and bizarre fictional literature that has no connection to the Bible or reality in general. No
wonder the world rolls its eyes.

The modern homeschool movement within evangelicalism is
another example of our unique subculture. To be clear, I've no problem with homeschooling in general. My own family utilized this
educational model for a time. How parents choose to educate their
children is none of my business. Public, private, homeschool…what-
ever. Certain parents are far more qualified to educate their children than are their local schoolteachers. Many parents are passionate
about it. Furthermore, given the inept school system in this country and the often dangerous conditions within many school districts,
homeschooling is a very feasible and often necessary option. I get
this. (Sorry for all the qualifiers, but I know how zealous people can
be about schooling choices.)

But when homeschooling is viewed as a superior level of spiritual
commitment or as a way to keep our kids from corruption, we're not
thinking biblically about the church, our kids, or the family.

Obviously, Christian parents (or morally conservative secular parents for that matter) cannot fulfill their roles faithfully if they simply
throw their children to the cultural wolves. Preparing our children
for the world ahead of them by exposing them to biblical models

of thought creates sound judgment and helps them live as believers. This commitment to forging their worldview will create a level of discernment as they face the unbiblical and anti-Christian agendas awaiting them. All of this is fine and good. But are we preparing our children to engage the culture with the gospel or simply to preserve a way of life handed down to them by their forefathers? "Christianity" and "family values" are not synonyms.

The real problem with our kids is not the culture, but their sin. The biggest threat to their souls is not that they will lose their innocence but that they will assume they are innocent to begin with. According to the Bible, they are not. They are just as sinful and corrupt as the very people we work so hard to protect them from. Our children are in danger when they assume they are Christian by virtue of their parents' choice of schooling. The recent family-integrated church movement—in its more extreme forms—has not lessened the confusion here. The family is not more important than the church. Family is important, but temporary. The church and the gospel are permanent.

> But this I say, brethren, the time has been shortened, so that from now on those who have wives should be as though they had none; and those who weep, as though they did not weep; and those who rejoice, as though they did not rejoice; and those who buy, as though they did not possess; and those who use the world, as though they did not make full use of it; for the form of this world is passing away (1 Corinthians 7:29-31).

The goal of Christianity and the church is not to protect our kids or families from the culture. To resist evil is just good common biblical sense. But Christianity is about planting the gospel deeply in our kids' lives so they can be redeemed, radically transformed, and sent into the culture with transformative power. Our Christian isolationism is completely incompatible with the gospel of grace and the mission of Jesus Christ.

> I am no more in the world; and yet they themselves are in the world, and I come to You. Holy Father, keep them in

Your name, the name which You have given Me, that they may be one even as We are. While I was with them, I was keeping them in Your name which You have given Me; and I guarded them and not one of them perished but the son of perdition, that the Scripture might be fulfilled.

But now I come to You; and these things I speak in the world so that they may have My joy made full in themselves. I have given them Your word; and the world has hated them, because they are not of the world, even as I am not of the world. I do not ask You to take them out of the world, but to keep them from the evil one. They are not of the world, even as I am not of the world. Sanctify them in the truth; Your word is truth. As You sent Me into the world, I also have sent them into the world (John 17:11-18).

As Jesus made explicit, it's not about escaping the world. It's about withstanding its pressure so we can infiltrate. Our version of church so conflicts with Jesus's prayer for us. Our convictions keep us from having a truly biblical worldview. When we pass our neighbors Sunday on our way to church—washing their boats and mowing their yards—what is our gut reaction? "Look at those pagans. They're going to hell." Who knows? They may actually be lost. But it's our next thought that betrays our confusion about the church. "They should be in church on Sunday." No they shouldn't. Why would they? They're lost (presumably). They are spiritually blind to the need for church. The church should go to them. Pull your car over and help them rinse off their Hummer. Until we conquer this misunderstanding, we've effectively cut ourselves off from the very mission field we were called to reach. Being in church does not save anyone.

Not long ago, I was invited to speak at a church over a weekend. The pastor was an amazingly gracious and hospitable man of God. Seriously, he and his congregation went out of their way to take care of me. The people were beyond friendly and welcoming. A bond of love characterized the fellowship. As the pastor drove me to church on Sunday morning, we saw his neighbor in full golf regalia loading his clubs into his SUV.

I had been wrestling with my own attitude toward the lost, so I caught myself. Seriously, it's tough not to go there. "Byron, you don't know the condition of that man's soul until you ask. Playing golf on Sunday is no indication of his eternal destiny. Why not assume that everyone needs to hear the gospel—even those who look saved and are at church 30 minutes early?" I've been programmed to respond in this manner my entire life and hate this attitude in me.

Right before I preached, the pastor stepped up to make announcements and welcome the congregation. When he did he said something along these lines. "On the way to church this morning I noticed one of my neighbors heading off to play golf. How sad is that? I'm so glad I'm here at church worshipping with the saints of God! There's no place I'd rather be."

There was a smattering of amens. My heart sank. I've heard this kind of rhetoric from pulpits through the years. I've heard it from my own pulpit. A statement like this tells you all you need to know about someone's view of the church. The very idea is a subtle yet substantial denial of the grace of God. We are no better before God than the Sunday golfer. Not even if we have flawless church attendance. We are righteous before God because an innocent Lamb was slain for us. We're sinners. We're at church because we (by God's grace) realized we are no better than this man or any other person on the planet. His sovereign grace is the supreme cause of our redemption. We go to church to thank God for His indiscriminate grace and to prepare ourselves for Monday, when we walk across the street to talk to the golfer. At some point in our lives we were as blind as he (if indeed he is).

My point is not to condemn my comrade in arms. I fight the same inclination in myself. Besides, for all I know, he has evangelized the golf guy. My point is to expose our misunderstanding of church and turn it toward a more biblical direction. What if that same tenaciously gracious spirit I saw in this congregation were turned on the culture? What if their love for each other were surpassed only by their love for the lost? (Indeed it may be. After all, what can you learn about a church from one visit?) What if they didn't come to hide from the world on Sunday but to reload their grenades for Monday?

The constant pounding of sovereign grace in the church transforms the church and makes it the world-tilting force it should be. The awareness of God's mercy in our own lives makes us automatically think of ways to reach the Sunday golfer rather than condemn him. It's the only force powerful enough to conquer our self-righteousness. It alone can keep us from boasting.

> But God, being rich in mercy, because of His great love with which He loved us, even when we were dead in our transgressions, made us alive together with Christ (by grace you have been saved), and raised us up with Him, and seated us with Him in the heavenly places in Christ Jesus, so that in the ages to come He might show the surpassing riches of His grace in kindness toward us in Christ Jesus. For by grace you have been saved through faith; and that not of yourselves, it is the gift of God; not as a result of works, that no one should boast. For we are His workmanship, created in Christ Jesus for good works, which God prepared beforehand so that we would walk in them (Ephesians 2:4-10).

Therefore, grace can never become common or cheap in our midst. We must always be in awe of what God has done and is doing. Otherwise we will never be the church.

The Outrageous Implications of Grace

Grace comes complete with some rather outrageous conclusions. I'm not sure many Christians have thought through the innumerable implications resident within the gospel of grace that we proclaim. We may believe and affirm it in theory, but we've yet to grasp how disturbing the corollaries of grace actually are. Once you begin to consider the repercussions of God's unconditional love of unworthy sinners, you immediately realize that an isolationist view of church conflicts with the message we were called to preach.

For instance, if grace is true (and it is), then we are no better than the worst person we can imagine. This reality confronts our "us and them" outlook on the world. There is only us. "All have sinned." Furthermore, if grace is true (and it is), then the reason you're a part of Christ's church has nothing to do with any intrinsic quality within you. God's choice of you was not based on any relative goodness. You were saved by grace. This means you are not more worthy of God's love because you were better than your neighbor—you know, the woman having an abortion.

Eventually, when you chase all these implications down, you begin to realize how wrongheaded our view of church can become. We're not better because we are in the church. We're in the church because we're sinners saved by grace. That's what the church is. A gathering of people saved from the muck of their sinful existence. The church is not a place to hide from the world. It should be the other way around. Grace is so radically powerful in our lives, the world can't possibly hide from us. When you preach sovereign grace consistently and unapologetically, the church becomes the church. But once you get over grace as an individual, your Christianity will fade into a vague spiritual oblivion, or your self-righteousness will make you mean and surly. Once we get over grace in the corporate setting, we will never find ourselves on the front lines of the lost. We'll try to avoid them. Church will be about hanging on till Jesus gets back.

Not long ago a new neighbor moved in near my family. Not an unusual event in our neighborhood. All seemed normal until a few days later when we received a registered letter from the gentlemen. The basic message was "Don't set foot on my property, or I'll take legal action." We live in one of those "zero lot line" developments. The families are right on top of each other, so the warning was a little puzzling. As strange as the note seemed, we gave the guy the benefit of the doubt and did our best to comply. But this posture became more and more difficult as the oddities escalated over the following weeks.

First, an emergency generator was installed on the outside of his house. Odd, but not an unheard part of homeownership in the States. It was the half-dozen cameras placed on the exterior walls of his house that raised our eyebrows. They were the black half-dome kind that rotate 180 degrees. The very ones you find in stores and public places. Then came the sensors all throughout his yard. They create an invisible net across the entirety of his property. They make an annoying buzzing sound whenever someone gets within five feet of his property or when you pull into your own driveway. Strange stuff, right? But wait—it gets even better.

The next thing to appear were some amazing security lights at the corners of his roof. Seriously, they are straight out of some sci-fi movie. When they come on, it looks like that spaceship scene from *Close Encounters*. They're initiated by movement. When they are engaged, they rise up from a dormant position and fix a beam of light onto the object that triggered it. The entire block lights up like the middle of the day. They actually follow you around. I feel like the lead singer for an '80s rock band when I step outside at night.

All of this made those characters on *Doomsday Preppers* look like amateurs. This guy has created a virtual fortress. He never comes outside. He never leaves. It's a mystery (and, quite frankly, none of my business).

I greeted the gentleman when he first moved in and attempted to have a neighborly relationship with him. Obviously, that did not last long. But I did try. There were several attempts. One day I noticed a Rottweiler puppy in his backyard. An awesome dog. I walked over near his yard and the dog came up to the fence. A nub where a tail once existed was going back and forth. I said something like "Hey there, fellah." You know, dog talk, but in a masculine voice.

The owner immediately said, "He's not that kind of dog."

He had my full attention at this point. "Really? What kind of dog is he?"

"An attack dog." I laughed out loud. We live on a cul-de-sac filled with kids. I thought he was joking, but he was dead serious. It was immediately awkward. I could not let the absurdity of this moment go unnoticed, so I said the first thing that came to mind. "Well, be careful around my nine-year-old. He's not a normal kid. He's an attack kid." And then I walked away. Baffled.

Weeks later my son informed me his brand-new soccer ball was in this man's yard. Indeed it was. But it was on the edge of his yard. Part of it was on the adjoining neighbor's property. I walked over to the adjacent neighbor's yard and picked the ball up. It was around nine thirty at night during the summer. No lights came on. No alarms went off. I thought I was in the clear. I felt like a secret agent.

Two days later a letter arrived. It had a time stamp on it at the very moment I picked up the ball. This time the message was even more explicit. "If you come into my yard again there is great potential that you will receive bodily harm, and I will not be responsible for your injuries." Basically, we will live near each other, but I will do anything necessary to avoid you. Got it.

I wonder sometimes if this isn't the very message the church delivers to the world around us. We see you out there and know you exist, but we've no intention of lowering the drawbridge. You're not getting in here, and we're not coming out there. Good luck finding hope.

Box Lunches in Pagan Territory

And again He went out from the region of Tyre, and came through Sidon to the Sea of Galilee, within the region of Decapolis (Mark 7:31).

And He directed the people to sit down on the ground; and He took the seven loaves and the fish; and giving thanks, He broke them and started giving them to the disciples, and the disciples gave them to the people. And they all ate and were satisfied, and they picked up what was left over of the broken pieces, seven large baskets full. And those who ate were four thousand men, besides women and children (Matthew 15:35-38).

Scholars have spent a lot of time arguing over the authenticity of this event. It seems strange to some that this miracle of mass feeding would occur just a few weeks after a similar one (see Matthew 14:15-21). The feeding of the 5000 and the feeding of the 4000 are nearly identical, so many readers have concluded that this one is invented by a scribe for some unknown reason. Obviously, if we hold a high view of the inspiration of the Scriptures, we can't agree with this conclusion. We believe it occurred just as it is recorded in the Bible. But how do we explain it? Why do we find this miracle performed the same way twice in just a few weeks?

Well, it is not exactly the same. In some ways this is a miracle of a completely different kind with an amazing effect.

The real miracle here is that God's grace extended to places the Twelve had never considered. Up until this moment, they believed God was present with a specific type of people (the Jews) in a very specific location (Israel). That is all they had ever known. But these are Gentiles, and this is pagan territory. This was outside the natural boundaries of their perspective. They were very, very far from home. The feeding of the 5000 was about God's grace to His chosen race. The feeding of the 4000 was about God's grace to the chosen from every other race.

The miracle here is that God's love and power were at work in such a strange place. It's the same supernatural act but with a completely different audience. This is exactly the point Jesus was intending to get across to these men. They had to get a grip on the true expanse of God's grace in the world. God's work in the world was much bigger than they had ever imagined. He was at work and intended to reveal himself in places they had never considered. When it came to what God was doing in the world, they couldn't see the forest for the trees. They had one version of God's work. They had not yet connected their calling to the rest of the world.

These men were no different from us. We too have one version—an American one. But God's work is so much more expansive than we realize. There is so much more than our version of church. In order to get the real perspective of our lives and the purpose of the church in God's economy, we must get a constant dose of the big picture. We are part of something amazing.

Hanging out in Gentile territory for the better part of a month would have been a serious shock to the system of a traditional Jew. These men had probably never ventured this far from home or from the temple courts. They were way out of their comfort zone. Mark informs us of their exact location. They were in the region of the Decapolis. That is about as far as you could get from the comforts of home. No Jew ever went out here. The Decapolis was a federation of ten Roman cities on the border of Palestine. It was at the very eastern end of the Empire. It was utilized by the Romans to extend their culture into the farthest reaches of their kingdom. Each city functioned as a satellite of the capital, complete with its politics, philosophies, morals, and basis of society. It was a thoroughly secularized beachhead of pagan culture.

Somewhere in the midst of these pagan cities Jesus sits down and begins to minister, just as He had done in the Promised Land to the promised people. "And large crowds came to Him, bringing with them those who were lame, crippled, blind, mute, and many others, and they laid them down at His feet; and He healed them" (Matthew 15:30).

"Those" people start coming to Him by the thousands. Within moments and for three days, the disciples are pressed up against the very people they had been conditioned to avoid. This would have been such a very unnerving experience for these men. Unclean people were everywhere. The disciples' comfort zone had been obliterated. We all have levels of comfort that limit our influence for Jesus and the gospel. The suburbs are a comfort zone of sorts. We use them as excuses for why we don't engage the world with the gospel.

The basic life strategy of most Jews was to preserve Hebrew tradition and keep it from the influence of the world. They were extremely exclusive. The basic goal was to avoid contact with the rest of the world. Preserve the culture. But in order to be obedient in following Jesus, His followers would have to abandon the thought that the rest of their lives would be spent hiding from the rest of the world. From this point forward, isolationism would no longer be acceptable as a life strategy. It was too self-absorbed to accomplish God's plans. God did not intend to shelter them. Hiding from the world in perfect environs was no longer going to cut it.

This background is what makes this scene so radical. Before, in order for unworthy people to get a crumb from the table of God's people, they were expected to go where God was. But now they saw God going to where they were. Grace had come out to uncharted places. The world no longer posed a threat to their way of life. Rather, their way of life posed a threat to that of the world.

> You are the light of the world. A city set on a hill cannot be hidden. Nor does anyone light a lamp and put it under a basket, but on the lampstand, and it gives light to all who are in the house. Let your light shine before men in such a way that they may see your good works, and glorify your Father who is in heaven (Matthew 5:14-16).

We Christians have our own version of this same tendency. We are taught pretty consistently that we are supposed to keep ourselves out of range of the world. We shelter ourselves and try to hold on until Jesus gets back. We design our lives, homes, kids, education, hobbies, and so on so they are out of the world's reach. The world is something we are to keep ourselves safe from. I'm pretty certain Jesus intended that we should be posing a threat to the world. Life was meant to be more than protecting our way of life.

The feeding of the 5000 took place in a day. The feeding of the 4000 develops over three days. These desperate people stick with Jesus for three long days. Who would want to leave? They were afraid grace might never come this way again. In all that time, the Twelve never consider the people's need. Jesus waited three days, but they never mention it. In some respects, the chosen people had become less than human. They had been conditioned over centuries with extremely deep prejudices. They themselves were a different class of people. Who they were made them more deserving of God's grace.

Their prejudice limited the extent of God's compassion. They had a one-size-fits-all way of thinking about God. From their religious perspective, everyone on the outside looked the same.

That was never going to cut it out here in the Decapolis. God's love was available even to outsiders. The disciples judged the lot of humanity on superficial criteria, and as a result they barely lifted a hand to help them. Like the disciples, we won't talk to certain types of people. We avoid them in public. We choose the seats farthest from people of certain races, cultures, lifestyles, looks, and so on. Those prejudices inhibit our mission. Jesus will have none of this from His church.

A Rejoinder

The Bible is not a spiritual handbook.

> Beginning with Moses and with all the prophets, He explained to them the things concerning Himself in all the Scriptures (Luke 24:27).

Morality is not a Christian worldview.

> Beware of practicing your righteousness before men to be noticed by them; otherwise you have no reward with your Father who is in heaven (Matthew 6:1).

Family values are not synonymous with Christianity.

> If anyone comes to Me, and does not hate his own father and mother and wife and children and brothers and sisters, yes, and even his own life, he cannot be My disciple (Luke 14:26).

Christianity is spiritual, but spirituality is not Christianity.

> God is spirit, and those who worship Him must worship in spirit and truth (John 4:24).

Humanitarianism is not the chief aim of the church.

> Jesus answered them and said, "Truly, truly, I say to you, you seek Me, not because you saw signs, but because you ate of the loaves, and were filled" (John 6:26).

Christianity is not about being happy but does result in joy.

> Consider it all joy, my brethren, when you encounter

various trials, knowing that the testing of your faith produces endurance (James 1:2-3).

You cannot find God's will for your life (in the popular sense) in
the Bible.

> I urge you, brethren, by the mercies of God, to present your
> bodies a living and holy sacrifice, acceptable to God, which
> is your spiritual service of worship. And do not be con-
> formed to this world, but be transformed by the renewing
> of your mind, so that you may prove what the will of God
> is, that which is good and acceptable and perfect (Romans
> 12:1-2).

Being a Christian is not about being a good person.

> There is none righteous, not even one; there is none who
> understands, there is none who seeks for God; all have
> turned aside, together they have become useless; there
> is none who does good, there is not even one (Romans
> 3:10-12).

You will not have your "best life" in this existence.

> Then the dust will return to the earth as it was, and the
> spirit will return to God who gave it. "Vanity of vanities,"
> says the Preacher, "all is vanity!" (Ecclesiastes 12:7-8).

God may not want you to be rich. He may want you to be poor.

> Listen, my beloved brethren: did not God choose the poor
> of this world to be rich in faith and heirs of the kingdom
> which He promised to those who love Him? (James 2:5).

Wealth is not a sign of God's favor.

> Now the poor man died and was carried away by the
> angels to Abraham's bosom; and the rich man also died
> and was buried. And in Hades he lifted up his eyes, being
> in torment, and saw Abraham far away, and Lazarus in his
> bosom (Luke 16:22-23).

Much contemporary Christian music isn't.

> But may it never be that I would boast, except in the cross of our Lord Jesus Christ, through which the world has been crucified to me, and I to the world (Galatians 6:14).

Many Christian books aren't.

> For if I preach the gospel, I have nothing to boast of, for I am under compulsion; for woe is me if I do not preach the gospel (1 Corinthians 9:16).

You don't need Jesus to be happy.

> For as in those days before the flood they were eating and drinking, marrying and giving in marriage, until the day that Noah entered the ark, and they did not understand until the flood came and took them all away; so will the coming of the Son of Man be (Matthew 24:38-39).

Struggling with sin is a normal part of the Christian life.

> If we confess our sins, He is faithful and righteous to forgive us our sins and to cleanse us from all unrighteousness. If we say that we have not sinned, we make Him a liar, and His word is not in us (1 John 1:9-10).

Moral or affluent people need the gospel just as much as immoral or poor people.

> One of the criminals who were hanged there was hurling abuse at Him, saying, "Are You not the Christ? Save Yourself and us!" (Luke 23:39).

America has never been a Christian nation.

> The kings of the earth and the great men and the commanders and the rich and the strong and every slave and free man hid themselves in the caves and among the rocks of the mountains; and they said to the mountains and to the rocks, "Fall on us and hide us from the presence of Him who sits on the throne, and from the wrath of the Lamb;

for the great day of their wrath has come; and who is able
to stand?" (Revelation 6:15-17).

The rich young ruler would not have been saved if he had sold
everything.

> For by grace you have been saved through faith; and that
> not of yourselves, it is the gift of God; not as a result of
> works, so that no one should boast (Ephesians 2:8-9).

Suffering is a normal part of life and not something to be escaped.

> For we know that the whole creation groans and suffers
> the pains of childbirth together until now. And not only
> this, but also we ourselves, having the first fruits of the
> Spirit, even we ourselves groan within ourselves, waiting
> eagerly for our adoption as sons, the redemption of our
> body (Romans 8:22-23).

Preaching from the Bible doesn't ensure faithfulness to the Bible's
message.

> He said to them, "These are My words which I spoke to
> you while I was still with you, that all things which are writ-
> ten about Me in the Law of Moses and the Prophets and
> the Psalms must be fulfilled." Then He opened their minds
> to understand the Scriptures (Luke 24:44-45).

Austere living is not a sign of spiritual devotion.

> Therefore let no one act as your judge in regard to food or
> drink or in respect to a festival or a new moon or a Sab-
> bath day—things which are a mere shadow of what is to
> come; but the substance belongs to Christ. Let no one keep
> defrauding you of your prize by delighting in self-abasement
> and the worship of the angels, taking his stand on visions
> he has seen, inflated without cause by his fleshly mind
> (Colossians 2:16-18).

The gospel is not about escaping hell or getting to heaven.

> If while we were enemies, we were reconciled to God
> through the death of His Son, much more, having been
> reconciled, we shall be saved by His life. And not only this,

but we also exult in God through our Lord Jesus Christ, through whom we have now received the reconciliation (Romans 5:10-11).

He who sits on the throne said, "Behold, I am making all things new." And He said, "Write, for these words are faithful and true." Then He said to me, "It is done. I am the Alpha and the Omega, the beginning and the end" (Revelation 21:5-6).

Culturally relevant messages are often disconnected from the actual point of the Bible.

The word of the cross is foolishness to those who are perishing, but to us who are being saved it is the power of God (1 Corinthians 1:18).

God did not save you because you have intrinsic value.

You were dead in your trespasses and sins, in which you formerly walked according to the course of this world, according to the prince of the power of the air, of the spirit that is now working in the sons of disobedience. Among them we too all formerly lived in the lusts of our flesh, indulging the desires of the flesh and of the mind, and were by nature children of wrath, even as the rest. But God, being rich in mercy, because of His great love with which He loved us, even when we were dead in our transgressions, made us alive together with Christ (by grace you have been saved), and raised us up with Him, and seated us with Him in the heavenly places, in Christ Jesus, so that in the ages to come He might show the surpassing riches of His grace in kindness toward us in Christ Jesus (Ephesians 2:1-7).

Preaching about a need for biblical preaching is not biblical preaching.

For my part, I am eager to preach the gospel to you also who are in Rome. For I am not ashamed of the gospel, for it is the power of God for salvation to everyone who believes, to the Jew first and also to the Greek (Romans 1:15-16).

There is no difference between local and world missions.

> He said to them, "Go into all the world and preach the gospel to all creation" (Mark 16:15).

Vegetables can't sing.

> Jesus answered, "I tell you, if these become silent, the stones will cry out!" (Luke 19:40).

You are not a better person for having become a Christian.

> It is a trustworthy statement, deserving full acceptance, that Christ Jesus came into the world to save sinners, among whom I am foremost of all. Yet for this reason I found mercy, in order that in me as the foremost, Jesus Christ might demonstrate His perfect patience as an example for those who would believe in Him for eternal life (1 Timothy 1:15-16).

You should not pattern your life after Joseph, David, Daniel, or any other biblical character.

> All have sinned and fall short of the glory of God (Romans 3:23).

Jabez only wanted some land.

> Now Jabez called on the God of Israel, saying, "Oh that You would bless me indeed and enlarge my border" (1 Chronicles 4:10).

Church is not where you go to escape the influence of the world.

> Go therefore and make disciples of all the nations, baptizing them in the name of the Father and the Son and the Holy Spirit, teaching them to observe all that I commanded you; and lo, I am with you always, even to the end of the age (Matthew 28:19-20).

God does not love you more if you read your Bible and pray.

> Therefore there is now no condemnation for those who are in Christ Jesus (Romans 8:1).

Sinners (even the worst you can imagine) are not your enemies.

> I say to you who hear, love your enemies, do good to those
> who hate you, bless those who curse you, pray for those
> who mistreat you. Whoever hits you on the cheek, offer
> him the other also; and whoever takes away your coat, do
> not withhold your shirt from him either (Luke 6:27-29).

Church attendance is not a sign of faithfulness to Christ.

> Many will say to Me on that day, "Lord, Lord, did we not
> prophesy in Your name, and in Your name cast out demons,
> and in Your name perform many miracles?" And then I will
> declare to them, "I never knew you; depart from Me, you
> who practice lawlessness" (Matthew 7:22-23).

A Christian president will not save our country or the world.

> God highly exalted Him, and bestowed on Him the name
> which is above every name, that at the name of Jesus every
> knee will bow, of those who are in heaven and on earth and
> under the earth, and that every tongue will confess that
> Jesus Christ is Lord, to the glory of God the Father (Phi-
> lippians 2:9-11).

"Having devotions" is not an indicator of spiritual discipline.

> The Lord said, "Because this people draw near with their
> words and honor Me with their lip service, but they remove
> their hearts far from Me, and their reverence for Me con-
> sists of tradition learned by rote..." (Isaiah 29:13).

The best thing you can do for morally upright people is assume
they are lost.

> When Jesus heard this, He said to him, "One thing you still
> lack; sell all that you possess and distribute it to the poor,
> and you shall have treasure in heaven; and come, follow
> Me" (Luke 18:22).

Finding your purpose in life is not the most important thing you can do.

> He said to him, "'You shall love the Lord your God with all your heart, and with all your soul, and with all your mind.' This is the great and foremost commandment" (Matthew 22:37-38).

Placing your faith in your parent's religion is damning.

> Bear fruit in keeping with repentance; and do not suppose that you can say to yourselves, "We have Abraham for our father"; for I say to you that from these stones God is able to raise up children to Abraham (Matthew 3:8-9).

Schooling choices are not signs of spirituality or good parenting.

> He gives a greater grace. Therefore it says, "God is opposed to the proud, but gives grace to the humble" (James 4:6).

Freedom of religion may not be good for Christianity.

> Only give heed to yourself and keep your soul diligently, so that you do not forget the things which your eyes have seen and they do not depart from your heart all the days of your life; but make them known to your sons and your grandsons (Deuteronomy 4:9).

"Christian movies" has become a punch line.

> Worthy are You, our Lord and our God, to receive glory and honor and power; for You created all things, and because of Your will they existed, and were created (Revelation 4:11).

Atheists can be "good" people too.

> If you love those who love you, what credit is that to you? For even sinners love those who love them. If you do good to those who do good to you, what credit is that to you? For even sinners do the same. If you lend to those from whom you expect to receive, what credit is that to you? Even sinners lend to sinners in order to receive back the same amount (Luke 6:32-34).

Principles for living taken from the Bible are often distortions of the Bible.

> Jews ask for signs and Greeks search for wisdom; but we preach Christ crucified, to Jews a stumbling block and to Gentiles foolishness, but to those who are the called, both Jews and Greeks, Christ the power of God and the wisdom of God (1 Corinthians 1:22-24).

Legislating morality is not helpful.

> "'But in vain do they worship Me, teaching as doctrines the precepts of men.' Neglecting the commandment of God, you hold to the tradition of men." He was also saying to them, "You are experts at setting aside the commandment of God in order to keep your tradition" (Mark 7:7-9).

Knowing the gospel is not evidence of believing it.

> You believe that God is one. You do well; the demons also believe, and shudder (James 2:19).

No one has been a Christian his entire life.

> If you confess with your mouth Jesus as Lord, and believe in your heart that God raised Him from the dead, you will be saved; for with the heart a person believes, resulting in righteousness, and with the mouth he confesses, resulting in salvation (Romans 10:9-10).

Abortion is not what's wrong with America.

> The heart is more deceitful than all else and is desperately sick; who can understand it? (Jeremiah 17:9).

Jesus would be confused in many of our church services.

> I looked, and I heard the voice of many angels around the throne and the living creatures and the elders; and the number of them was myriads of myriads, and thousands of thousands, saying with a loud voice, "Worthy is the Lamb that was slain to receive power and riches and wisdom and might and honor and glory and blessing."

And every created thing which is in heaven and on the earth and under the earth and on the sea, and all things in them, I heard saying, "To Him who sits on the throne, and to the Lamb, be blessing and honor and glory and dominion forever and ever."

And the four living creatures kept saying, "Amen." And the elders fell down and worshiped (Revelation 5:11-14).

Christ is hard to find in most Christian bookstores.

I am not ashamed of the gospel, for it is the power of God for salvation to everyone who believes, to the Jew first and also to the Greek. For in it the righteousness of God is revealed from faith to faith; as it is written, "But the righteous man shall live by faith" (Romans 1:16-17).

Second Chronicles 7:14 has nothing to do with America.

As for you, if you walk before Me as your father David walked, even to do according to all that I have commanded you, and will keep My statutes and My ordinances, then I will establish your royal throne as I covenanted with your father David, saying, "You shall not lack a man to be ruler in Israel" (2 Chronicles 7:17-18).

Being angry at sinners for being sinners is not a sufficient evangelism strategy.

God so loved the world, that He gave His only begotten Son, that whoever believes in Him shall not perish, but have eternal life. For God did not send the Son into the world to judge the world, but that the world might be saved through Him (John 3:16-17).

Notes

Introduction

1. D.A. Carson, *The Cross and Christian Ministry* (Grand Rapids: Baker Books, 1993), 26.

Chapter 1: Suburbianity: Lies, Myths, and Suburban Legends

1. Timothy Keller, *Counterfeit Gods* (New York: Dutton Adult, 2009), 1, 3.

Chapter 2: The Truth Hiding in the Wide Open

1. The quotes are from these books by Deepak Chopra: *The Book of Secrets* (New York: Three Rivers Press, 2004), 1-2, 203; *Creating Affluence* (Novato: New World Library, 1998), 63-64; *The Seven Spiritual Laws of Success* (Novato: New World Library, 1994), 93, 30; *Power, Freedom, and Grace* (New York, Three Rivers Press, 2006), 6-7, 82-84; *The Path to Love* (New York, Three Rivers Press, 1997), 87-88.

Chapter 7: Hanging On Until Jesus Gets Back

1. D.A. Carson, *Becoming Conversant with the Emerging Church* (Grand Rapids: Zondervan, 2005), 50.

2. Thom Rainer and Eric Geiger, *Simple Church* (Nashville: B&H Books, 2006), 19.

Also from Byron Forrest Yawn...

What Every Man Wishes His Father Had Told Him

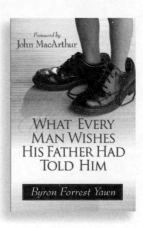

Every man encounters significant struggles in life, resulting in poor choices and decisions. Frequently these mistakes can be traced back to a common problem—a father who (often unintentionally) failed to provide counsel or a positive role model.

In *What Every Man Wishes His Father Had Told Him*, Byron Yawn offers vital input many men wish they had received during their growing-up years. This collection of 30 simple principles will help you to...

- identify and fill the gaps that occurred in your upbringing
- benefit from the hard-earned wisdom of others so you don't make the same mistakes
- prepare your own sons for the difficult challenges of life

Byron presents 30 truths that are based in Scripture and vital for your life, including affection, courage, balance, consistency, and more.

To learn more about Harvest House books and
to read sample chapters, log on to our website:

www.harvesthousepublishers.com

HARVEST HOUSE PUBLISHERS
EUGENE, OREGON